ADAPTABLE

ADAPTABLE

How to Create an Adaptable Curriculum
and Flexible Learning Experiences
That Work in Any Environment

A.J. JULIANI

Adaptable: How to Create an Adaptable Curriculum and Flexible Learning Experiences That Work in Any Environment
© 2021 A.J. Juliani

This book is available at special discounts when purchased in quantity for educational purposes or for use as premiums, promotions, or fundraisers. For inquiries and details, contact the publisher at books@impressbooks.org.

Published by IMPress, a division of Dave Burgess Consulting, Inc.
IMPressbooks.org
DaveBurgessConsulting.com
San Diego, CA

Library of Congress Control Number: 2021947861
Paperback ISBN: 978-1-948334-40-2
Ebook ISBN: 978-1-948334-41-9

Cover design by Rina Pal
Interior design by Liz Schreiter
Edited and produced by Reading List Editorial
ReadingListEditorial.com

To all the students who taught me more
than I could ever teach them.

Contents

Introduction

LEARNING IN AN EVER-CHANGING WORLD

Blockbuster was doing everything right. They had a fantastic business. They were booming with strong year-over-year growth. They would tweak something here or there. Improve customer service. Move to DVDs or Blu-ray. But the model stayed the same. Because in all honesty, the model was working.

Here was the model, in the simplest terms:

- People want cheap entertainment.
- People want convenient entertainment.
- People want quick entertainment.

Blockbuster's job was to give the people what they wanted (at scale). Netflix came along and challenged Blockbuster by telling customers they didn't have to go to the store anymore. Netflix would send the DVDs right to your house for a monthly flat fee. A lot of people liked this. They could go online, pick out the movies and TV shows to add to their queue, and have a steady flow of DVDs coming in throughout the month.

Blockbuster said, "We can do that too!" But you all know this is not how the story ends. By the time Blockbuster had caught onto Netflix's model, they had already changed how it worked. Netflix moved their entire business model to meet the growing needs of people who wanted to stream movies and shows to their devices.

Here was the Netflix model, in the simplest terms:

- People want cheap entertainment.
- People want convenient entertainment.
- People want quick entertainment.

Netflix's goal was to give the people what they wanted (at scale). See the difference?

- Cheap entertainment in 2013 was eight dollars a month, not three dollars for every movie you rent.
- Convenient entertainment in 2013 was a large collection of titles at your house or anywhere you had an internet-connected device, not going down to the local store and hoping your movie was in stock.
- Quick entertainment in 2013 was as fast as your internet connection, not renting movies, watching them only on devices that had a DVD player, and returning them on time.

The difference is simple: Netflix saw how the world was changing around them and adjusted accordingly. They weren't doing something "better," instead they were doing something "different" because it matched what was actually happening in the world.

A MODEL THAT WORKS SOMETIMES NEEDS TO BE CHANGED

I get a bit frustrated when I hear (over and over again) that education needs to be completely overhauled. That we need to change the entire system. That nothing works.

I often talk with teachers who are giving their best every single day. In the midst of the daily practice of teaching and leading, they see that the world is changing, our students are changing right along with it, and we have a responsibility to move our practice forward as well.

This *doesn't* mean we abandon what has worked well in the past. It only means we need to think critically about how it can be adjusted to work well today.

When Socrates wanted to create an engaging learning experience for his students, he had to focus on an experience that was human, social, meaning-centered, and language-based. These four principles of learning still work today. But how those principles of learning look in practice sure seem different now than they did ten, twenty, or one hundred years ago.

Our principles can stay the same over time, but our practices must adapt and transform along with the times.

A question we can consistently ask is: How can we think and act like Netflix if we have been Blockbuster for so long? To me, this is the big question. I'm not saying schools are like businesses (because they are not). I'm also definitely not saying students are like consumers (because they are not). Instead, let's take this lesson and apply it to our schools with a focus on change. Here are some questions I'm asking right now, and they are questions that need to be asked every year:

- How can we shape our learning activities and assessments to match what the world actually looks like right now (not in the future)?
- How can we create a curriculum cycle that is flexible and adaptive enough to allow for doing things differently each year if need be?
- How can we focus on student-centered learning opportunities all of the time instead of some of the time?

Netflix isn't a perfect model to look at, but we can take one thing away from their story: they have changed their working model with the world instead of fighting back at it. In order to continue to be adaptable we have to try and do the same thing in education. We must teach differently, because our world is different today than it was last year, and it's going to be different next year as well.

PART 1

AN ADAPTABLE

CURRICULUM

·1·

PEOPLE OVER PROGRAMS

Here is a big mistake I made for many years: I thought I knew what was best for students, for learning communities, and for educational organizations. Not all the time and not in every situation, but often I believed I had a good take on what was best in learning experiences.

But because of my limited experience, I had a limited worldview. Even as that experience has grown over time, I still don't know what is best for every student.

And that is OK.

That, actually, should be our starting point for creating a curriculum. Yes, we have standards. Yes, we still have to deal with those standardized tests and college admissions processes that are outdated and not supported by research. Yes, we want each and every student to have a quality education experience. Yes, we want students to gain the fundamental skills and knowledge they need to be successful in and out of our schools.

But curriculum needs to be adaptable. It needs to be flexible. It needs to support the idea that our students need windows, mirrors, and sliding doors in their lessons, activities, resources, and assessments. The curriculum needs to be malleable and resilient.

If the entire school has to shift to remote learning, the curriculum should support that shift. If an individual classroom or student needs to go hybrid, the curriculum should not be any less worthy than if they were fully in-person.

How though, you may be asking, can we do this? How is this possible in the ever-changing landscape of education? A simple step in making this a reality is to focus on the *people*, not the *programs* when designing a curriculum and, ultimately, learning experiences.

I remember when Lyn Hilt wrote, "It's people, not programs."[1] Isn't this the truth? How often do schools, teachers, and administrators buy in to a program or tool, thinking (hoping, praying) it will be the golden ticket to improved reading scores or math fact fluency or a more positive school climate? Too often.

In March 2020 when the COVID-19 pandemic began and forever changed education, those programs were not adaptable. The people were.

Those textbooks were not flexible in March 2020. The teachers were.

Those assessments were not resilient in March 2020. The educators were.

Now, over a year removed from the start of everything changing in education, we are at a crossroads. Many schools are back in-person, many are in a hybrid/concurrent/parallel situation with some students at home and some in school, and some are still remote, depending on the situation in their community.

Whatever happens in the next few months or years, one thing remains true: we will have to be adaptable, as we always are as educators. When we look at our current outdated curricula, will we start with the people or the programs? When we look at our assessments and performance task redesigns, will we start with the people or the programs? When we talk about what worked, what didn't, and what we want to keep, cut, and create, will we start with our students, our communities, our teachers, and our people, or the programs?

You can look at all the research you want, but the people in education already know what the research is going to tell you because we live it and see it every day. We know the culture of testing doesn't create or lead to more achievement.[2] It is why there has been a groundswell of educators creating and using performance tasks for years. We know many of our texts, resources, and materials are outdated and not relevant to our students. It is why there has been a movement around open education resources (OER) and teacher-created resources that work for our kids. We know the curriculum can't be static, not all standards are important, and the human and social side of learning is what we have to focus on first before the content is ever relevant. We've been doing the work. You've been doing the work. The people have been doing the work.

In order to create an adaptable curriculum that works for every student, we have to start with our people and listen to our students and community. We need to build it from the ground up and invest the time and energy into developing something that works. If we choose to *rely on a program* instead of using resources, materials, and programs to *support our people*, then we'll always be playing from behind. When the curriculum is developed by your teachers for your community of learners, then (I know it sounds crazy) it works for your students.

This is hard work. Right now, most of us in education are just trying to stay afloat. We've seen many of these underlying issues bubble to the surface even more once the pandemic hit.

It takes time to develop an adaptable curriculum. It takes time to develop meaningful performance tasks. It can't be solved by buying a program or singular resource. And, as ASCD points out, the most notable successes occur in schools and districts whose teachers build their own, admittedly imperfect, curriculum.[3]

Maybe we have to go slow to go far. Maybe it will take longer for the people to do the work under the current circumstances, but the alternative just won't cut it.

Give me people over programs every single day. It's not even a debate.

And if we are going to put people first, that means relationships have to be a priority over everything else in education.

RELATIONSHIPS > EVERYTHING ELSE IN EDUCATION

My grandmom is wise. And at ninety-six years old, she's still as curious as ever. A few months ago, we were having a discussion about the work we are doing in my school district and my thoughts on where education and learning are going in the future.

The questions were fascinating, but even more so was the dialogue. She asked me whether or not I thought the increasing use of devices was taking away from face-to-face conversations like the one we were having. We engaged in a back-and-forth on the pros and cons of having so much attention put on our phones and technology.

But this was not a one-sided debate where I was trying to convince her of the benefits of technology. Grandmom is still as active as ever, working in both the US and England throughout the year while often traveling to Spain (and sometimes India) to do mission work. Medical issues have slowed her down over the years, but not for long—she keeps moving, talking, and traveling more than most of us do!

She built an email list over the years (way before it was cool to build an email list) and regularly communicates with her friends, family, and those interested in the work she is doing. She has seen the power of technology to connect people, but she also realizes that it is often a "starting place" for relationships or a "continuing" place for information.

Then she hit me with the quote that I was thinking about all night: "It all comes back to relationships. Whether you use technology or have face-to-face conversations, it has to be about building that relationship if anything different is going to happen."

Boom. Drop the mic, Grandmom!

GREAT SCHOOLS AND GREAT TEACHERS FOCUS ON RELATIONSHIPS

I've been lucky enough to be in some amazing schools and teacher classrooms over the past few years. Without fail, the most consistent trait I see in each of these places is a focus on relationships. The relationships come from having opportunities for inquiry, challenging students, solving problems together, and doing work that is meaningful. But they also come from small side conversations, moments in the hallway, supporting each other outside of the classroom, and taking longer than expected to talk about an issue in class.

There has been a tremendous amount of pressure put on teachers and administrators to focus on everything else in education. The focus has been ramped up on data, differentiation, and individualized instruction. Yet, we can talk about all the data we want, but it won't make a difference if you don't have relationships with those teachers, and if those teachers don't have relationships with their students.

We can keep changing instruction and curriculum all we want, but as the late, great Rita Pierson said in her now famous TED Talk:

> A colleague said to me, "They don't pay me to like the kids. They pay me to teach a lesson. I should teach it. They should learn it. Case closed."
>
> Well, I said to her, "You know, kids don't learn from people they don't like."
>
> She said, "That's a bunch of hooey."
>
> And I said to her, "Well, your year is going to be long and arduous, dear."[4]

It's not only with the kids that relationships matter. It's with all of us. Think of the best teachers you've had. Think of the best leaders you've had. Think of the best colleagues you've had. In my case, they all put the focus on relationships first and everything else second.

It's easy to get caught up in the "future of learning" and miss out on what has always worked when it comes to learning: relationships.

Yet, in our current world, relationships can look very different. The human and social lens of learning has never been more important, but there have also never been more ways to build, sustain, and cultivate a relationship around learning.

HOW ARE WE BUILDING RELATIONSHIPS?

Gary Vaynerchuck, CEO of VaynerMedia, best-selling author and investor, put this into perfect perspective when talking about relationships built with technology:

> I'm humbled by all the interaction I have with you guys through this phone. . . . So many hate the phone and feel like it hurts us . . . I don't . . . I look at it as the new pen and paper . . . No one gets mad if you wrote a letter to a friend or a family member . . . I do that 100s of times a day . . . Too many caught up in the tool that creates the communication instead of what it is enabling . . . I wouldn't have known 99.999999% of u [sic] if we were living our current ages 40 years ago . . . That's amazing and I'm excited and happy to have a chance for you to read this #community[5]

Here are some questions to think about how we use today's technology and modes of communication to build relationships:

- Are you using today's technology to build learning relationships?
- Are you meeting kids where they are?
- Are you meeting teachers where they are?
- Are you meeting families where they are?

The future of learning is a lot like the past of learning; it centers around the human, or social, side of curiosity, creativity, and adaptation. But the one thing that is very different is how many avenues we have for reaching and growing this side of learning. Grandmom said it right: the focus on relationships should never change, even if the way to build those relationships does change.

PEOPLE FIRST

Throughout this book we will focus on how to create an adaptable curriculum. We will look at strategies and structures for flexible learning experiences. We will dive into the research and studies that support this work. There will also be step-by-step guides and actionable takeaways in each chapter. However, if we do not put the people and the relationships first, then all of that work will be for nothing.

Chapter 1 is all about the people. If we want schools to be successful right now, and in the future, we will always have to focus on the people. If we want to support our students as learners, we will always have to first see them as people.

Let's do that first; everything else can follow. Then, and only then, will we have a foundation for meaningful learning to happen across grade levels, departments, and all areas of our communities.

·2·

HUMAN

Windows, Mirrors, and Sliding Doors

In 1990, Dr. Rudine Sims Bishop published an essay about the importance of providing young readers with diverse books that reflect the "multicultural nature of the world" in which we live.

In the essay, Dr. Bishop coined the phrase "windows, mirrors and sliding glass doors" to explain how children see themselves in books and how they can also learn about the lives of others through literature. Here is how she puts it:

> Books are sometimes windows, offering views of a world that may be real or imagined, familiar or strange. These windows are also sliding glass doors, and readers have only to walk through in imagination to become part of whatever world has been created or recreated by the author. When lighting conditions are just right, however, a window can also be a mirror. Literature transforms human experience and reflects back to us, and in that reflection,

we can see our own lives and experiences as part of a larger human experience. Reading, then, becomes a means of self-affirmation, and readers often seek their mirrors in books.[1]

CREATING CURRICULUM WITH PURPOSE

As a former middle-school and high-school teacher, instructional coach, curriculum administrator, and director of learning, I've been part of a number of curriculum revisions that sought to bring a variety of multicultural books and authors into the classroom. When I spoke with Erica Buddington (CEO of Langston League) on *The Backwards Podcast*, we chatted about some of the mistakes I made along the way, as well as the important work Erica is doing at Langston League to make curriculum (not just books) mirrors, windows, and sliding doors.

Erica Buddington founded the Langston League, a multi-consultant curriculum firm that specializes in teaching educators to design and implement culturally responsive instructional material and professional development. Their clients include Google's Code Next, Medgar Evers College, Harlem Children's Zone, Movers & Shakers, Achievement First Schools, Reconstruction US, and many others. Erica has been a Brave New Voices slam champion, an HBO Def Poet, and has spent a decade in the classroom. Erica is also the author of four books and has been featured on *The Steve Harvey Show*, *Forbes*, BuzzFeed, *Black Enterprise*, and more.

We had the chance to talk with her about curriculum, her current work at Langston League, and her *Decolonized* YouTube series. The focus of Erica's current work with Langston League is to create mirrors. To be specific, a curriculum full of mirrors.

And as Dr. Bishop goes on to say in her essay, this work is for all of our students:

Children from dominant social groups have always found their mirrors in books, but they, too, have suffered from the lack of availability of books about others. They need the books as windows onto reality, not just on imaginary worlds. They need books that will help them understand the multicultural nature of the world they live in, and their place as a member of just one group, as well as their connections to all other humans.[2]

So, how do we do that? How do we create a curriculum that goes beyond programs, textbooks, and "standards" that often lead schools right back to those same programs and textbooks that support test-prep?

As Erica Buddington mentioned on *The Backwards Podcast*, this is hard work.[3] Not only is it hard work, but it also takes serious time to develop an adaptable curriculum. Buddington explains how they start the curriculum work at Langston League by getting to know the community where the curriculum is being created. They work with the community, with the students, the families, and the educators to create a curriculum with a purpose.

A DIFFERENT (AND RELEVANT) CURRICULUM

Every school should have a different curriculum because every school community is different. This doesn't mean that resources can't be used across schools and communities. Of course they can. But, if we want to create a curriculum with a purpose, we must first, and most importantly, define what the purpose is of the learning experiences we are crafting for K–12. This is outlined by authors McTighe and Wiggins in their Understanding by Design framework for curriculum development:[4]

1. **Identify Desired Results:** These are the transfer-learning goals that drive the assessments we will use as well as the choice of resources, texts, and experiences that will guide the process.

2. **Determine Acceptable Evidence:** How will we know our students understand? How can they share their learning? What does this look like? What performances and products will reveal evidence of meaning-making and transfer? What additional evidence will be collected for other desired results?

3. **Learning Plan:** What activities, experiences, and lessons will lead to the achievement of the desired results and success at the assessments? How will the learning plan help students with acquisition, meaning-making, and transfer? How will the unit be sequenced and differentiated to optimize achievement for all learners?

The identifying desired results step is where you can take the expectations of the state standards and combine that with your goals and purpose as a community of learners. Each of these questions should have different answers depending on your purpose and community:

- What long-term transfer goals are targeted?
- What meanings should students make?
- What essential questions will students explore?
- What knowledge and skills will students acquire?

As Buddington so aptly points out, this process takes time. However, Langston League has seen tremendous success with its process of creating mirrors. More than 90 percent of the students that take part in their workshops and engage with their materials request their organization again.

So that is what we are looking for in a curriculum. One that serves as windows, mirrors, and sliding doors for all of our students. One that supports the local community and the greater global good. One that starts with a purpose and ultimately leads to authentic, meaningful, and relevant learning experiences across grade levels, subjects, and classrooms.

HOW TO CRAFT A CURRICULUM THAT FOCUSES ON PEOPLE AND NOT RESOURCES

If you are anything like me, your typical curriculum process goes in four- to six-year cycles. This was based on making sure schools had money for textbooks in their budget. Year one would be an ELA curriculum rewrite and purchase, year two would be math, and so on.

While there are many problems with this cycle approach, the main one is that things change much too quickly for a four- or six-year timeline to review, revise, and update curricular documents. To combat this problem, we want to focus on creating organic curriculum that is adaptable. The goal is to tweak, update, and modify curricular documents on the fly, throughout the year, and each summer so they are truly living and breathing guides.

We can do this in a simple three-step process.

1. IDENTIFY THE DESIRED RESULTS AND THE GOALS OF THE COURSE, SUBJECT, OR GRADE LEVEL FOR THE STUDENTS.

These desired results should not necessarily change throughout the year but can be modified as needed.

Here is where you need to include the community and students in the process. We can't accurately identify results without including them in the decision making. The curricula resources, performance tasks, activities, and lessons will be pointing in the direction of these desired results.

2. CREATE PERFORMANCE TASKS.

In this step you must create, develop, or find performance tasks (assessments) that allow students to demonstrate their knowledge and understanding and reach the desired results.

Each semester, teachers and students can reflect on what worked well (and what did not) with the performance tasks. They can be modified or changed for future years, and they can serve as an indicator on future assessment types, allowing educators to make changes prior to starting upcoming units.

3. THE EVER-CHANGING LEARNING PLAN.

Developing a learning plan for your class is not enough. I've met teachers that start fresh every year and create new lessons. I've also met teachers who reuse the same lessons over and over, year after year.

Neither of these practices is inherently bad, or wrong. However, the only way to know whether or not to create a new learning plan, tweak an existing plan, or reuse a previous plan is to look at how well the lesson currently (in the moment) and previously (last year or in a previous class) prepares students for their performance tasks. This is the art of teaching. We can get all of the diagnostic results we want, but it is up to the teacher to change, modify, and create based on what they are seeing from their class.

When students are actively engaged in the act of learning something new and able to demonstrate a clear understanding of that skill or knowledge, then we know we've got a learning plan that works.

A final, additional step would be to check for transfer. How well are the concepts that students are learning being transferred to new situations and different contexts? Transfer is where we see the real gain from learning, as the knowledge is being applied to new and unique situations.

TRANSFER

Learning for Right Now
and the Future

The first time I met Esther Wojcicki (affectionately called "Woj" by almost everyone that knows her), we started talking about a serious issue that is common across all levels of education. Esther, who had been teaching for well over thirty years, said, "Most classes tell you exactly what you need to learn, how to learn it, and then ask you to share what you've remembered (or memorized) only to spit it back on a test the exact way it was laid out previously in a lecture."

"However," she went on to say, "most jobs don't work that way. Most of life doesn't work that way. We are constantly asked to problem solve, work with others to find solutions, and create rather than memorize."

Yes, I thought. *I had seen this, too, as a teacher. What we did in many of my teaching and learning experiences didn't quite match up to the reality of work and life.*

It wasn't until later in the conversation that I found out why Esther was so passionate about this topic, and consequently I was soon asking her to take my own kids for a "Camp Esther."

It turns out Esther Wojcicki is famous for three things: teaching a high school class that has changed the lives of thousands of students; raising three daughters who have each become famously successful as the CEO of YouTube, the founder and CEO of 23andMe, and a top medical researcher; and inspiring many others in Silicon Valley and around the world.

Esther's methods are the opposite of helicopter parenting. Her work as a teacher and parent are the result of TRICK—Esther's secret to raising successful people: Trust, Respect, Independence, Collaboration, and Kindness.[1] She believes in enabling teenagers to pick projects that relate to their own passions and to the real world, and providing them with the independence to discover the steps to complete them. Above all, she wants to encourage parents to let their child lead while remaining a guide on the side.

Our first conversation was seven years before she authored *How to Raise Successful People*, but our discussions since then have been as much about my own kids growing up as they have been about our students' experiences in schools around the world.[2]

Esther is also the founder of the media arts program at Palo Alto High School, where she built a journalism program from a small group of twenty students in 1984 to one of the largest in the nation including six hundred students, five additional journalism teachers, and nine award-winning journalism publications. She also serves as vice chair of Creative Commons and has previously worked as a professional journalist for multiple publications.

COMPETENCE AS A GOAL OF INDEPENDENCE

One of the areas I struggle with as a parent (and as a teacher) is when and how to give independence to my kids. Whether in class or while my kids play with friends, there is so much control and compliance that is assumed in the roles of parent and child or teacher and student.

I asked Esther about the *I* in TRICK—which stands for Independence—and why it was so important. She said that independence is important when it leads to competence. That should be the goal of independence. If you are allowing your child to cook and make food by themselves, the goal is that at some point in time they will feel competent to do this in a situation without the parent present. If you are encouraging your child to go to the store or walk to a friend's house without you, then you are hoping that this will lead to a sense of competence.

"Throughout life we all have moments," Esther told me, "that require us to feel competent at figuring something out, even though we don't have the exact steps or plan laid out for us."

This too should be a goal in school. Understanding is revealed when students can transfer their learning to new and "messy" situations. This is life. In and out of school. Taking what we have experienced and learned and transferring that to new situations.

IF TRANSFER IS THE GOAL, HOW DO WE PREPARE FOR IT?

Jay McTighe has made some very clear distinctions about the role of performance tasks (versus tests) to promote transfer:

> A performance task is any learning activity or assessment that asks students to perform to demonstrate their knowledge, understanding and proficiency. Performance tasks yield a tangible product and/or performance that serve as evidence of learning. Unlike a selected-response item (e.g., multiple-choice or matching) that asks students to select from given alternatives, a performance task presents a situation that calls for learners to apply their learning in context.
>
> Performance tasks are routinely used in certain disciplines, such as visual and performing arts, physical education, and career-technology where performance is

the natural focus of instruction. However, such tasks can (and should) be used in every subject area and at all grade levels.[3]

This aligns with Esther's work and focuses on independence. Independence gives an opportunity to learn and be competent for a performance later that day, that year, or in life.

Have you ever wondered why kids ask "When am I going to use this in life?" It is often because the only way they are assessed is through a selected-response item test. They don't see many adults spending their days taking tests; thus, the question makes sense.

I hated hearing this question as a teacher because the goal of what we were learning in my class was a transfer of what we did in school to what they do in life. However, this was not always shared with students, and I made the mistake time and time again of not including students in this process.

THE TRICK IS TO FOCUS ON TRANSFER

McTighe shares some characteristics of performance tasks that promote transfer (there are additional examples in his full article):[4]

- Performance tasks call for the application of knowledge and skills, not just recall or recognition.
- Performance tasks are open-ended and typically do not yield a single, correct answer.
- Performance tasks establish novel and authentic contexts for performance.
- Performance tasks provide evidence of understanding via transfer.
- Performance tasks are multi-faceted.
- Performance tasks can integrate two or more subjects as well as twenty-first-century skills.

- Performances on open-ended tasks are evaluated with established criteria and rubrics.

The key to making any performance task relevant and meaningful is to be able to fail at the performance task and continue learning. Performance tasks can fall into the same category of tests if they are not authentic. As McTighe points out, "While any performance by a learner might be considered a performance task (e.g., tying a shoe or drawing a picture), it is useful to distinguish between the application of specific and discrete skills (e.g., dribbling a basketball) from genuine performance in context (e.g., playing the game of basketball in which dribbling is one of many applied skills)."[5]

This is why we need to take a closer look at Esther's principles of TRICK: Trust, Respect, Independence, Collaboration, and Kindness.

Esther's five-point guidance comes in the form of principles, not rules, which means that unlike much parenting advice, it spans many years—from getting babies to sleep to how to react when they grow up and trash the house.

It boils down to loving your kids for who they are, not who you want them to be, and getting out of the way as much as you can. Children are more able than parents may realize, and in need of more space to grow than their parents are willing to give.

Esther focuses on a simple and often shared mantra of our time: let kids fail (the test, the piano exam, the tryout, the whatever). "Kids are supposed to screw up as kids so they screw up less as adults," she writes, noting that most teachers know that failure is integral to learning.[6]

Whether at home or in school, we have to bring trust, respect, independence, collaboration, and kindness into the curriculum and performances that share learning—even when things are not perfect. This means going beyond the standards. It means teaching above the test. And above all, it means that learning is a process and performances get better with time, they get better with practice, and ultimately, they can lead to a real transfer of skills and understanding in the world.

MAKING THE JUMP TO TRANSFER

Forgive the curriculum nerd in me, but *transfer* is one of the most important topics in education that we rarely talk about. We know it matters, we design entire curricula with the goal of transfer, but in the daily grind of teaching and learning, we can often go months without having a conversation about *transfer*.

What is transfer? Here is how authors Julie Stern, Krista Ferraro, Kayla Duncan, and Trevor Aleo define it in their new book, *Learning That Transfers: Designing Curriculum for a Changing World*: "Learning Transfer: Using our previous learning to understand or unlock a completely new situation."[7]

This is generally the goal of education. Not to "prepare" our students for something that we can foresee but, instead, to help them to prepare themselves for situations neither of us could predict. As we talk about transfer, we need to focus on a quote from early in *Learning That Transfers*: "As educators, we need frameworks that allow us to respond to changes without constantly overhauling or reinventing everything that we do."

CAN WE REALLY DESIGN LEARNING THAT TRANSFERS?

The answer is a resounding yes. However, even with that emphatic yes, this work can only be done intentionally. The authors of *Learning That Transfers* argue that not only can we teach for transfer but we can also do so while teaching "less."

What if we selected the most powerful, transferable, organizing ideas from our curricular documents, and anchored everything we explored in those concepts? Could this help educators turn off the conveyor belt of "covering" an endless list of objectives while also ensuring students are prepared to tackle topics they encounter without a teacher's guidance? Yes, it can. We can both teach less and prepare our students to tackle more.

To do this, we can use a simple framework for teaching concepts and their connections. Enter ACT: The Learning Transfer Mental Model.[8]

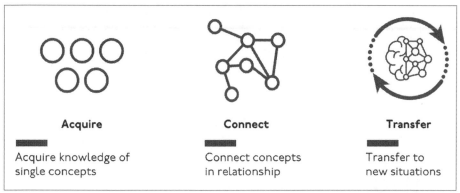

Acquire

Acquire knowledge of single concepts

Connect

Connect concepts in relationship

Transfer

Transfer to new situations

Source: Stern, Ferraro, Duncan, Aleo, 2021

ACT is a powerful way to reframe the learning process.

Step 1: Design learning experiences that help students acquire knowledge of single concepts.

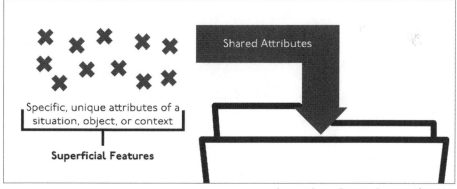

Shared Attributes

Specific, unique attributes of a situation, object, or context

Superficial Features

Source: Stern, Ferraro, Duncan, Aleo, 2021

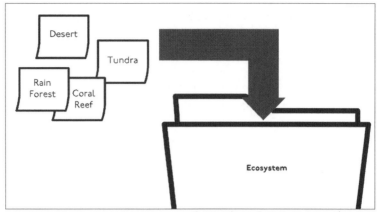

Source: Stern, Ferraro, Duncan, Aleo, 2021

Step 2: Connect those concepts in a relationship.

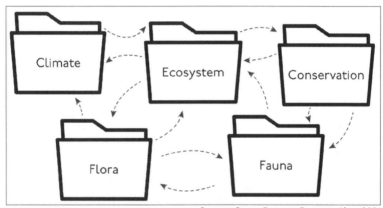

Source: Stern, Ferraro, Duncan, Aleo, 2021

Step 3: Transfer those concepts and connections to new situations.

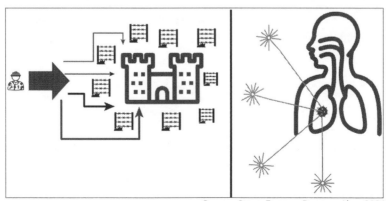

Source: Stern, Ferraro, Duncan, Aleo, 2021

WHAT STRATEGIES CAN WE USE TO PROMOTE TRANSFER?

The authors of *Learning That Transfers* do a fantastic job of breaking down some questions we can ask to develop transfer strategies in their book:

1. **Recognize the concepts that apply:** Which concepts are at play in this situation?

2. **Engage prior understanding of the conceptual relationship:** What do I already know to be true about the relationship among these concepts? What specific examples support my understanding?

3. **Determine the extent to which prior understanding applies:** What makes this new situation different from the situations I've seen in other learning? Does what I understand about the relationship between these concepts apply to this new situation? Which parts of my prior understanding transfer and which don't?

4. **Modify and refine understanding based on the new situation:** How has transferring to this situation refined or reshaped my thinking?[9]

Along with these questions, we can focus on seven shifts that also help develop transfer throughout the learning process:

Shift #1: Students	1. The role of the student is directors of their own learning.
Shift #2: Teachers	2. The role of the teacher is designer of transfer-focused lessons.
Shift #3: Curriculum	3. The goal of the curriculum is to build transferable, organizing schema of both disciplinary and modern literacies.
Shift #4: Instruction	4. Instruction honors students' prior knowledge and experiences to foster conceptual connections that transfer.

Shift #5: Assessments	5. Assessments are a system of feedback about the quality of teaching and learning.
Shift #6: Leaders and Parents	6. Parents and school leaders partner with teachers on the long-term growth of students so that they can live meaningful lives.
Shift #7: Community	7. Community members collaborate with teachers so that students can transfer their learning to real-world situations.

Source: Stern, Ferraro, Duncan, Aleo, 2021

TAKING THE NEXT LOGICAL STEP

Here's the key to putting a focus on transfer in the classroom: You don't have to do it all.

Maybe you are not part of the curriculum writing process. In that case, focus on the next logical step for you and your students: designing transfer-focused lessons around concepts and connections.

Maybe you are on a committee looking at the role of tests in our schools. Then focusing on assessment is your next logical step.

You can't possibly do all seven of these shifts at once. And, depending on your role, you may not have any control or influence over some of these shifts. The goal is to take the next logical step of focusing on transfer whenever possible. When we take the next logical step, our ability to adapt becomes easier because we stay in the moment, and thus we can be flexible with where we are and where we want to go.

·4·

PLAN

Develop Curriculum Using Design Thinking

I distinctly remembering learning how to type. It was hard. I had been a hunt and peck perfectionist up until age fourteen when my school provided a computer course focused on the keyboard.

My teacher would shout out commands as we feverishly tried to get our fingers in the right place.

"*A, S, D, F!*"

"*J, K, L,* semicolon!"

For a long time, I could still type faster by hunting and pecking. But, as I continued to practice, my words-per-minute count grew, and I was able to type without looking at the keyboard. By the end of that year, my hunting and pecking days were over. I had been successfully assimilated as a QWERTY typist, and I never looked back.

Interestingly, I never questioned the layout of QWERTY or where it came from. I assumed (I tend to do that) that it was designed for speed and thought this was the best it could get. Then I came across Nassim Nicholas Taleb's book, *Fooled by Randomness.* In one section,

Taleb brings up the QWERTY keyboard and the backward reason for how it was designed:

> The arrangement of the letters on a typewriter is an example of the success of the least deserving method becoming successful. Our typewriters have the order of the letters on their keyboard arranged in a non-optimal manner. As a matter of fact, in such a non-optimal manner as to slow down the typing rather than making it easier to type faster.
>
> This was done deliberately in order to avoid having the ribbons become jammed as they were designed for less electronic days of yore. Once we started to build better typewriters and computerized word processors, several attempts were made to change the keyboard in order to make them more efficient for typing purposes.
>
> All of these attempts failed. People had been trained on "QWERTY" keyboards and their habits were too sticky for change. This is called a "path dependent outcome" and it has thwarted many attempts at modeling or changing behavior.[1]

As Taleb points out, in 1874 when an American inventor named Christopher Latham Sholes first designed the QWERTY layout, its purpose was to keep the keys from jamming, not for speed, accuracy, or efficiency. Regardless of how the world changed, the QWERTY keyboard never got an update, because it worked "well enough" and people did not want to change.

DESIGNING FOR FUNCTION, NOT CHANGE

Sholes used the design-thinking process to develop the typewriter. He first started out by learning about current issues with other typewriter designs:

Sholes had been for some years developing the typewriter, filing a patent application in October 1867. However, the original key layout, with the second half of the alphabet in order on the top row and the first half in order on the bottom row, led to some problems. The keys were mounted on metal arms, which would jam if the keys were pressed in too rapid succession.[2]

Sholes then began to ask questions to understand the actual problem before creating a prototype:

Sholes's solution was separating commonly used letter pairings, such as "ST," to avoid these jams, effectively allowing the typist to type faster, rather than slower.[3]

Next, he focused on highlighting what was working and then fixing what was failing in his initial design. This iterative process brought about change that was again focused on solving the jamming problem:

He went through several design iterations, attempting to bring the typewriter to market. When he sold the design to Remington in 1873, the QWERTY layout looked like this:

2 3 4 5 6 7 8 9 –,
Q W E . T Y I U O P
Z S D F G H J K L M
A X & C V B N ? ; R[4]

Remington made several adjustments, and launched the Sholes and Glidden typewriter on July 1, 1874.[5] Its keyboard layout was almost the same QWERTY keyboard layout we use today, with a few minor differences. The numbers 1 and 0 were left out to help shave down production costs on the basis that these numerals could be produced using other keys, such as a capital I and a capital O. Remington also swapped the R and "." keys. The 0 was added fairly early on, but some keyboards well into the 1970s were still missing a 1.[6]

When this typewriter was launched to the world, it took a while to sell and needed some polishing in terms of the overall product before it hit a fit with the market. The first Remington typewriter sold poorly. It could only type in uppercase letters, was expensive (at $125 per unit), and often broke. The updated Remington 2 typewriter, introduced in 1878, changed this. Not only did it remedy some of the defects of the Sholes and Glidden machine, the launch allowed Remington to sell the typewriter business to three former employees.[7] Bringing marketing expertise to bear, the new Remington Standard Typewriter Company was able to bring the typewriter to commercial success.[8]

Today, most of the world still uses a QWERTY keyboard. We still teach QWERTY in our schools. And generally, no one questions how it was designed, who it was designed for, and why we still use the 1870 model almost 150 years later.

WHAT HAPPENS WHEN THE WORLD CHANGES?

There are at least six different keyboard layouts that are well-known enough to have a Wikipedia page.[9] Of these six, Dvorak is the one that has a small following of people that have run studies and research to show the benefits of this model over QWERTY:

> Though Dvorak may sound like another string of letters, it's in fact the surname of this keyboard layout's inventor, August Dvorak. The inventor felt, when he patented his design in 1936, that QWERTY was uneconomical and uncomfortable—and therefore wasn't the perfect layout. Dvorak believed that his layout was more efficient, and studies seem to agree.
>
> People using QWERTY keyboards only make 32 percent of strokes on the "home row" (where your fingers naturally rest on a keyboard). For Dvorak, that rises to 70 percent. And likewise, most people are right handed: Dvorak accounts for that, making more than half the strokes right

handed. QWERTY calls on people to use their left hands more. But save for a few eager practitioners, Dvorak is the lesser-known layout.[10]

The takeaway from how typewriters evolved (and didn't evolve) is that regardless of the benefits of Dvorak, people do not want to change when stuck in comfortable habits that work well enough. We can see a very similar pattern with our education system. Our current model was designed years ago with specific purposes in mind. A lot has stayed the same since that design, including when we go to school and when we have breaks from school, how many hours are spent learning each day, the subject areas that are taught, and the grade levels. This list could go on, but I think you get the point.

QWERTY was designed for a different world and different purpose, and although it still works fine (as I currently type on my QWERTY keyboard), that doesn't mean it is the best solution. There are many schools and districts that are moving away from a "traditional" education experience. In pockets across this country and the world, things are changing. Yet the majority of schools function in ways eerily similar to a nineteenth-century model.

In the design-thinking process, there is a piece that we often forget to continue with after launching it out into the world: iteration. If we don't consistently iterate, we will consistently fall behind. After launching a new idea into the world, iteration brings us back to a place where we can look, listen, and learn again.

The QWERTY keyboard was developed for a mechanical device that had problems with keys getting stuck. With digital devices, we don't have to worry about that problem anymore. So, let's look and learn about possible solutions to make it a better process.

Our educational system was developed for a time period of agriculture lifestyle and industrial growth. We are not preparing the majority of our students to work in fields or in factories anymore. So, let's look and learn about possible solutions to make it a better process.

USING THE DESIGN-THINKING PROCESS TO DEVELOP CURRICULUM

Design thinking provides a way to think about creative work. It starts with empathy—working to really understand the problems people are facing before attempting to come up with ideas and create solutions.

Where design thinking originated is a bit of a debate. Some claim that it started in the sixties with the Sciences of the Artificial.[11] Others point to Peter Rowe's 1987 book *Design Thinking*, which focused more on urban planning and architecture. Still others point to Robert McKim's work in Experiences in Visual Thinking.[12] Like all great ideas, it has been an evolution, influenced by thousands of people. We know that our work around design thinking has been influenced by people like Tom and David Kelley, Tim Brown, John Maeda, and Peter Rowe as well as organizations like Stanford d.school and IDEO.

There are several different interpretations of the phases in design thinking. Here are the phases of design thinking as shared by Stanford d.school:[13]

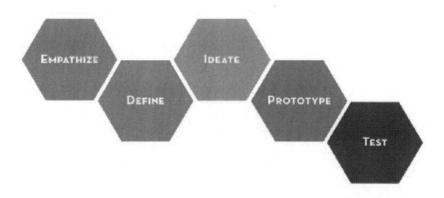

And there are other models, frameworks, and descriptions of the design-thinking phases from various organizations and universities:[14]

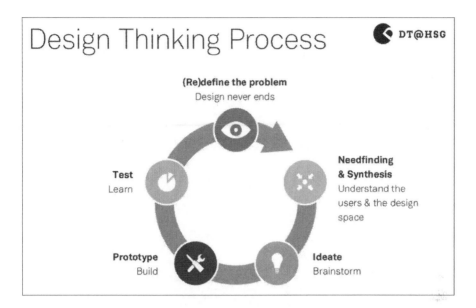

I began to use the design-thinking process during student-led inquiry projects like Genius Hour and 20 Percent Time, which led me to start helping other teachers structure their inquiry projects with choice around the design-thinking process. I saw the process as a new way to develop lessons, units, projects, and curriculum.

When I got into a conversation about design thinking with John Spencer (who was also using the process as a classroom teacher), we both agreed that the biggest struggle we had when using design thinking and sharing the process with other educators was its implications for K–12 schools.

What did we do about this problem? We began to try and solve it using the design-thinking process. We looked at the terminology used, the sample exercises and activities available, and how teachers and students responded to the different phases. We talked with teachers using design thinking in their classrooms and met with those that wanted a framework for creative work. Then we started to design and build out an idea. We highlighted what worked and kept on revising.

The end result was the LAUNCH Cycle, a K–12 framework for design thinking.[15] The LAUNCH Cycle is not a formula. It is not a step-by-step guide to being creative. However, we've used the LAUNCH

Cycle framework to make creativity an authentic experience time and time again in our classrooms and schools. It has been used across many schools, organizations, and institutions as a way to plan, develop, and build curriculum that is adaptable and flexible.

DESIGN THINKING IS USED (ALMOST) EVERYWHERE

Let's take a look at the growth of the term *design thinking* using Google's Ngram Viewer.

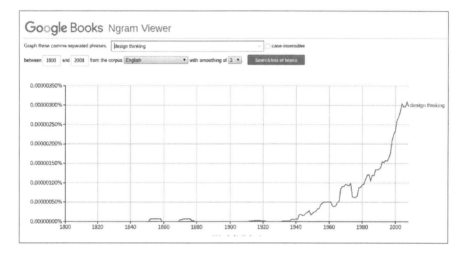

The term has jumped in explosive growth. Design thinking is used at universities, in organizations, by artists and designers, by engineers, and by many in the business and corporate world.

While design thinking was originally used in many cases to design products, it is now being used to tackle big problems in all kinds of sectors. David Kelley, who is the founder of the design firm IDEO as well as Stanford d.school's Institute of Design (and author of *Creative Confidence*), puts the benefits of design thinking into a simple statement:

> We moved from thinking of ourselves as designers to thinking of ourselves as **design thinkers**," he continues.

"What we, as design thinkers, have, is this creative confidence that, when given a difficult problem, **we have a methodology that enables us** to come up with a solution that nobody has before.[16]

Design thinking can be (and is) used by so many different industries because of this statement. It provides a methodology for creating innovative solutions to all kinds of difficult problems.

DESIGN THINKING HELPS CREATE FLEXIBLE LEARNING EXPERIENCES AND CURRICULUM

This is the interesting thing about design thinking. It can be used for entire-school problem-solving and for projects in a specific classroom.

At Mount Vernon School, they've embraced design thinking as a way to scale authentic learning in younger grades (K–5) and upper grade levels (6–12). They came up with a playbook that has been used all over the country. Here's how they introduce it:

In 2014, a team of MVIFI (Mount Vernon Institute for Innovation) designers embarked on a design challenge to scale the DEEP methodology into tools for design thinkers to use. Inspired by IDEO and Stanford's d.school, this playbook has been used all over the country in various industries to inspire people-centered problem solving. We have decided to offer this playbook, which includes a design thinking introduction called a Flashlab, free of charge under Creative Commons Attribution-NonCommercial-ShareAlike License.[17]

At Germantown Academy, a private school near Philadelphia, Director of Innovation Gaby Russomagno has worked with the staff to develop a design-thinking mindset. Then they brought this work to the entire school in a year-long challenge:

In the Upper School, "Challenge GA" will be implemented as a year-long House competition involving the entire student body and faculty. An issue concerning the GA community as a whole will be presented and each House will be charged with designing and presenting its own solution. Throughout the year, Houses will use House Meetings, occasional assemblies, and outside school time to research, design, and construct viable solutions to the problem. At the end of the year, during a special assembly in April, each House will present its solutions to a panel of professional judges. A winning resolution will be selected, and the GA community will then work to implement the solution.[18]

In each of these examples, an entire school, department, or classroom will go through the stages of the LAUNCH Cycle to identify and solve problems with unique solutions. Here are the phases as we look at them to develop curriculum:

L: LOOK, LISTEN, AND LEARN

In the first phase, staff and stakeholders that are developing curriculum look, listen, and learn. The goal here is awareness. It might be a sense of wonder at a process or an awareness of a problem or a sense of empathy toward an audience or group.

Creating or redesigning curriculum has to start with empathy. When we look at what we have on paper and compare it to what is happening in class, we get a sense of how the ideas and theories are being translated into actual practice and learning. When we listen to our stakeholders, students, community, and colleagues, we get a better sense of what matters, what is missing, and what is important. When we take time to learn what is needed, we are able to cut what is not necessary, add what is missing, and tweak what needs to be changed.

A: ASK TONS OF QUESTIONS

Sparked by curiosity, the curriculum team moves to the second phase where they ask tons of questions. They can share these questions with friends, teachers, mentors, and the world.

Typically, we begin the curriculum-planning process with a goal in mind of what we want to create or what we want to change to existing curriculum. Design thinking guides you to start with empathy, then take what you learned and ask lots of questions of various stakeholders. The questions can be about anything that came up in the first phase, and they should be asked without any expectation of what the answer might be.

U: UNDERSTANDING THE PROCESS OR PROBLEM

This leads to understanding the process or problem through an authentic research experience. The team might conduct interviews or needs assessments, research articles, watch videos, or analyze data. During this phase they are constantly putting their work out for others to look at and give feedback.

N: NAVIGATE IDEAS

The team then applies that newly acquired knowledge to potential curricular solutions. In this phase, they navigate ideas. Here, they not only brainstorm but they also analyze ideas, combine ideas, and generate a concept for what they will create.

C: CREATE A PROTOTYPE

In this next phase, the team creates a prototype. This is by no means a finished curriculum. It might be an entire unit or a yearlong overview of a course. It may include a performance task or series of lessons. The goal here is to make something that is not perfect but is malleable and ready to change based on feedback from the teachers leading the learning, and the learners involved in the unit, activity, or task.

H: HIGHLIGHT AND FIX

Next, the team begins to highlight what's working and fix what's failing. After their curriculum prototypes have been used by real students and teachers, feedback is critical to adapt the working curriculum plans and flesh them out into organic processes that are ready to be improved.

The goal here is to view this revision process as an experiment full of iterations, where every mistake takes them closer to success. As they share what they've made, the feedback they receive will be key to the revision process.

LAUNCH TO AN AUDIENCE

The prototype and revision process take time to continue to test and build. When the curriculum writing is done, it's ready to launch. In the launch phase, the curriculum is sent to an authentic audience—the staff, students, and stakeholders.

However, what makes the design-thinking process so critical in curriculum development is that once you launch the new curriculum, the process is not over. Every launch leads back to the first phase where the team and stakeholders look, listen, and learn. It is through this process that they will ask new questions, understand new problems and circumstances, and eventually, navigate ideas that can create new modifications and prototypes on top of and adjacent to the existing curriculum.

When we use design thinking to develop curriculum, the work is never finished, and the goal is to continue to iterate and improve year after year. When an event like the pandemic happens, the process is already in place to adapt, modify, and change what we are learning and how we are learning through the curriculum planning.

·5·

CREATE

Write Flexible Curriculum Maps with a Backward Process

I distinctly remember the moment I wanted to become a teacher. There was nothing fancy or profound about the moment, instead I had a feeling. I was going into my third year of college and was in between majors. I had been a business major, an accounting major, a history major, and had recently switched to an English major. (This was part of the reason it took me five and a half years to graduate but not the whole reason!)

West Chester University had a tutoring program for writers at a local high school. I was sitting in West Chester Henderson High School's "Writing Zone" working with a student who was writing a memoir. It was my fourth time at the school in the "zone" (as the kids called it), and I felt helpless. Nothing I said seemed to connect with the students. I talked above most of them and failed to make any impact in our short ten-minute sessions. I kept trying to help with their grammar, structure, and overall style, but it seemed all their questions were about content, so I answered as best I could. We all struggled through the process.

In the middle of this session, a young man walked in from the hallway. I had seen him before, but it looked as if he was heading straight to our table to talk with the young woman sitting across from me. He came right up to us, nodded a "Hi" to her and then to me, then said, "Hey, thanks so much for your help the other day. Just got back my paper, and Mrs. Reeves said it was my best yet." He flashed a B- grade my way.

We talked for a bit about the essay, and then he moved on to the back of the library to talk with some friends.

It was less than a thirty-second conversation. And it changed everything for me. I realized that even when I thought I was struggling and doing an awful job at helping these students, I could still make a difference. I realized that making a difference wasn't about helping that student get an A+. It was all about helping him get better.

My *why* for teaching was so simple: I could help people move from their point A to their point B. And I could help them even when I thought I wasn't being of much help.

Since then, I've had that same *why* as a teacher, coach, staff developer, school leader, professor, writer, speaker, and creator.

FINDING YOUR WHY

Simon Sinek, author of *Start with Why*, explains why it is so important to have this sense of "why" and purpose in what we do. He shares how it makes a difference for people and organizations just about everywhere:

> About three and a half years ago, I made a discovery. And this discovery profoundly changed my view on how I thought the world worked, and it even profoundly changed the way in which I operate in it. As it turns out, there's a pattern. As it turns out, all the great inspiring leaders and organizations in the world, whether it's Apple

or Martin Luther King or the Wright brothers, they all think, act and communicate the exact same way. And it's the complete opposite to everyone else. All I did was codify it, and it's probably the world's simplest idea. I call it the golden circle.

Why? How? What?

This little idea explains why some organizations and some leaders are able to inspire where others aren't. Let me define the terms really quickly. Every single person, every single organization on the planet knows what they do, 100 percent. Some know how they do it, whether you call it your differentiated value proposition or your proprietary process or your USP. But very, very few people or organizations know why they do what they do. And by "why" I don't mean "to make a profit." That's a result. It's always a result. By "why," I mean: What's your purpose? What's your cause? What's your belief? Why does your organization exist? Why do you get out of bed in the morning? And why should anyone care? As a result, the way we think, we act, the way we communicate is from the outside in, it's obvious. We go from the clearest thing to the fuzziest thing. But the inspired leaders and the inspired organizations—regardless of their size, regardless of their industry—all think, act and communicate from the inside out. They start with "Why."[1]

Let's think about this for a moment. When we meet someone, we often ask them *what* they do. During the conversation, we can sometimes get into *how* they do what they do. But we almost never get to the *why*.

As a society, we tend to shy away from having those deep conversations about our work and our purpose. We often assume there is a *why*, but for many, our occupation or work may only have a monetary value attached to the purpose.

In education, the *what* and the *how* emerge as students play the game of school. For our students, the *what* is the work they have to do in and out of school. Depending on how well they do the work assigned, they can ultimately have different post-secondary opportunities (i.e., college). They often say their *why* is college (or a career). But, as Sinek points out, this is a result (just as getting paid is a result of work) not the ultimate *why*.

When we live in a state of compliance, it is almost impossible to find your *why* and live it out. Compliance is the easy choice, not the better choice.

We must bring this same type of "why-first" thinking into our curriculum development process. When we know *why* we are developing a curriculum and *who* it is for, then we can have a better understanding of *how* it should be developed and *what* is important to include.

THE BIG QUESTION: WHAT ARE WE PREPARING STUDENTS FOR?

When we look around at what has happened since the COVID-19 pandemic, one thing is obvious: no one was prepared for this. As much as we'd like to say we prepare students for careers, we don't know what those careers will look like. As much as we'd like to say we develop curriculum that prepares students for college, we don't know what the higher-education landscape will look like next year, let alone five to ten years down the road. When we develop curriculum and learning experiences, our goal should be to help students prepare themselves for anything.

An opening question we typically ask during curriculum development is this: Are we raising, preparing, and teaching our students and children to be chefs or cooks?

Tim Urban explains the difference between a chef and a cook in his post for the blog *Wait But Why*. As you read his explanation, think about all the times you've acted like a cook versus a chef.

The words "cook" and "chef" seem kind of like synonyms. And in the real world, they're often used interchangeably. But in this post, when I say chef, I don't mean any ordinary chef. I mean the trailblazing chef—the kind of chef who invents recipes. And for our purposes, everyone else who enters a kitchen—all those who follow recipes—is a cook.

Everything you eat—every part of every cuisine we know so well—was at some point in the past created for the first time. Wheat, tomatoes, salt, and milk go back a long time, but at some point, someone said, "What if I take those ingredients and do this . . . and this . . . and this . . ." and ended up with the world's first pizza. That's the work of a chef.

Since then, god knows how many people have made a pizza. That's the work of a cook.

The chef reasons from first principles, and for the chef, the first principles are raw edible ingredients. Those are her puzzle pieces, her building blocks, and she works her way upwards from there, using her experience, her instincts, and her taste buds.

The cook works off of some version of what's already out there—a recipe of some kind, a meal she tried and liked, a dish she watched someone else make.

What all of these cooks have in common is their starting point is something that already exists. Even the innovative cook is still making an iteration of a burger, a pizza, and a cake.

At the very end of the spectrum, you have the chef. A chef might make good food or terrible food, but whatever she makes, it's a result of her own reasoning process, from the selection of raw ingredients at the bottom to the finished dish at the top.[2]

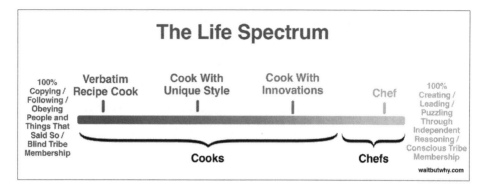

A cook is a follower. They can even be a creative follower, but they'll never create from their own understanding. Instead, they will always build on what others have done. A cook is often doing old things in new ways.

Chefs, on the other hand, are experimenting and doing new things in new ways. They are building and experimenting and often failing. A chef is doing new things in new ways.

Are we encouraging our kids to experiment like a chef? Are we supporting them when their efforts turn into "terrible" food? Do we only praise kids for cook-like efforts?

Chefs question the world around them. Chefs question answers as often as they answer questions. Yet, we often reward students for "cook-like" behaviors, while discouraging them from digging deep like a chef might do.

In fact, it's been documented that this not only happens to some children but to a huge population of kids as they grow up and become teenagers and adults. Couple that concept with what another favorite writer of mine, James Clear, explained recently on his blog:

> In the 1960s, a creative performance researcher named George Land conducted a study of 1,600 five-year-olds and 98 percent of the children scored in the "highly creative" range. Dr. Land re-tested each subject during five year increments. When the same children were 10-years-old, only 30 percent scored in the highly creative range.

This number dropped to 12 percent by age 15 and just 2 percent by age 25. As the children grew into adults they effectively had the creativity trained out of them. In the words of Dr. Land, "non-creative behavior is learned."

It makes sense, right? Creative thinking is a close cousin of first principles reasoning. In both cases, the thinker needs to invent his own thought pathways. People think of creativity as a natural born talent, but it's actually much more of a way of thinking—it's the thinking version of painting onto a blank canvas. But to do that requires brain software that's skilled and practiced at coming up with new things, and school trains us on the exact opposite concept—to follow the leader, single-file, and to get really good at taking tests. Instead of a blank canvas, school hands kids a coloring book and tells them to stay within the lines.[3]

Take a moment and think of your own life. Think of your own learning path. When did the term "learning" become synonymous with "school?" Why do students feel more stress centered around "learning" as they grow older? Why will students spend hours and hours of their own time learning how to create a virtual world in Minecraft but feel discouraged when given time to learn in school?

It's been quite apparent to me over the past two decades in public education as a teacher, administrator, and now parent that most of us are saying the right things. We want students to be creative. We want students to do innovative work. We want authentic learning tasks and assessments. We want to challenge our students to be problem solvers. But when most of us look at the practices in our own schools and our own homes, it looks much different than what we want.

So, how do we get from here (*wanting* school and learning to look a certain way) to there (school and learning *actually* looking the way we want it to look)?

I know I personally must admit that I've often taken the easy route. It's much easier to teach a class of cooks than it is a class of chefs. It's much easier to raise cooks than it is to raise chefs. It's much easier to tell my students and my own children that all will be OK if they follow this magic formula: Listen. Do what you are always told. Get good grades. Get into a good college. Get a good job. Have a good life.

The problem is that the magic formula doesn't work anymore, and I'm not sure it ever did. I know many adults who have followed that exact path and can't stand their job and complain about their life.

Ultimately, as parents, teachers, and leaders, we have to ask ourselves, "What is the purpose of all this schooling? What is the purpose for almost fifteen thousand hours of instruction and learning time in a school setting from K–12?"

Do we want to continue producing students who believe their life will be set as a cook? Or who want to live life like a chef?

THE BACKWARD APPROACH

If we can agree that part of our role in curriculum development is to prepare our students for the unknown, then you might say (as I did a few years ago), "What's the point then?" Honestly, with the world and education system changing so frequently, we are often stuck between trying to teach what was always taught and doing everything entirely new. But we can find common ground by using a backward design approach to develop adaptable curriculum. As Michelle Lia says in her NCEA brief *Universal Design for Learning: Getting Started with Backward Design*:

> We use Backward Design daily. If you cook, you decide what you will cook, what ingredients you will need, in which pot to cook it, for how long and so on. If you are a musician, before your set you decide which songs to play, in what order, when you will take a break, even what the lighting will look like. All of the tasks we do require us

to think ahead and plan. Why? So we get what we want. Teaching and learning is no different.[4]

Backward design is best used in curriculum development when pairing the process alongside universal design for learning (UDL). UDL is an education framework based on decades of research in neuroscience and endorsed by the Every Student Succeeds Act. UDL is considered best practice for teaching all students in an inclusive learning environment.

The goal of UDL is to create learners who are purposeful and motivated, resourceful and knowledgeable, and strategic and goal oriented, in other words—expert learners. With UDL, teachers transition their role to facilitator, removing barriers to learning by giving students options and choices that empower them to take control of their own learning and reach rigorous state standards. To universally design lessons, teachers must provide multiple means of engagement, multiple means of representation, and multiple means of action and expression. UDL can be explained in many ways, but I love the dinner party analogy my friend and *UDL Now!* author Katie Novak shares often in her workshops and on her blog:

> I like to explain the differences by asking teachers to think about hosting a dinner party. Let's say you have invited over thirty guests. Several of these guests have food allergies, another few are gluten-free, some are vegetarian or lactose intolerant, and your brother is exclusively Paleo. You want to be the perfect host, and you want to accommodate everyone.
>
> Scenario 1: You decide to make individual meals for each guest so that each of them has the perfect dish. That is a lot of juggling to do. In the end, you are exhausted from all of the cooking, made a few mistakes because it is nearly impossible to get everyone's individual meal perfect, and didn't enjoy yourself. At the same time, you are

frustrated that some of your guests preferred others' meals when you had made a special dish JUST FOR THEM.

What I just described is the dinner party equivalent of DI. DI is presenting options, but those options are directed by the teacher. For example, you may take one group of students aside and ask them to read an extra piece of literature because you can tell they are more advanced than their peers. You ask another student to draw a picture instead of writing an essay since you know writing is challenging for him. You are presenting options, but those options are governed by you and it's possible you haven't chosen the right options for the right students. You are burnt out from trying to create so many individualized lessons.

Scenario 2: Let's go back to the dinner party. Rather than preparing thirty individual meals, why not put out a buffet? Include lots of variety, but let the guests choose what is best for them, what they believe will work with their individual diets, and satisfy them. You don't witness guests peering at other's dishes wishing they had been given the same thing. You are relaxed and engaged. You have saved your energy for interacting with your guests, instead of wasting it preparing imperfect options.

UDL offers students a "buffet" of options. The options are offered by the teacher but they aren't individualized for specific students. Through the UDL framework, students are intended to become self-directed learners and choose the options that work best for them, not the other way around. With UDL, students learn to take responsibility for their learning. They are learning the "why" of learning as we turn on the affective network of the brain by providing multiple means of engagement. They learn the "what" of learning as we ignite the recognition network of the brain by providing multiple means of representation. And they learn the "how" of learning as we turn on the strategic network of the brain through multiple means of action & expression.[5]

Katie also shares that in education there is often a third scenario. This scenario is the "casserole" option where everyone is fed the same meal in one big pot. It doesn't matter what your dietary needs are or what your taste palette wants, when you have a casserole as your only option, that is what you get.

Pair this with the idea of one-size-fits-all lessons in the classroom. Every student, regardless of their needs (and wants) gets the same lesson, at the same pace, at the same level. Just as a casserole would be sure to miss the mark for many of your guests, the one-size lesson would look the same in the classroom.

UDL AND CURRICULUM DESIGN

When developing curriculum, we always start with the end in mind. What are the transfer goals? What are the standards? What do students need to understand and be able to do? How can they demonstrate those skills and knowledge?

Allison Posey of CAST, Inc. provides three guiding principles when bringing UDL into lesson planning and curriculum design in her article on Understood's website:

> UDL can transform your classroom practice. However, there is no "magic box" of tools and resources in a UDL classroom. Instead, when you integrate UDL, you'll notice the following:
> - **There is a strong focus on goals.** In a UDL classroom, there is a strong focus on learning goals for students. Teachers and students talk about why those goals matter and how they support challenging, meaningful

opportunities to learn. You'll also see students creating their own learning goals.

- **There is a focus on variability.** In a UDL learning environment, differences in experience, knowledge, and ability are expected. Flexible options are built into lessons for all students. That allows you and your students to talk about how different tools or resources support them as they work toward the goal. It also means not all of your students will be doing the same thing at the same time.

- **There is a focus on the barriers in the design of the environment.** In a UDL classroom, the focus is on how to change the design of the curricular goals, assessments, methods, and materials — not on how to "fix" the students. For example, you may have asked yourself, "Why aren't my students engaged?" UDL would encourage you to reframe the question: "How can the design of this lesson better engage students?"[6]

Here are some ways you can integrate UDL into your curriculum design while still focusing on the backward approach:

1. HIGH EXPECTATIONS AND GOALS WITH FLEXIBLE PATHS TO ACHIEVE THEM.

When we have high expectations of students, they are challenged to reach them. But if we don't have the scaffolds and supports for students, they can be overwhelmed by chasing after the same goals as everyone else and not seeing the same growth in the beginning.

Focus on providing flexible paths and ways for students to achieve those goals. This can be more time, a different way to consume the information (read, watch, listen, explore, etc.), and conferencing at checkpoints to see progress and answer questions.

2. VARIOUS PERFORMANCE TASKS THAT ASSESS THE SAME KNOWLEDGE AND SKILLS.

In the second half of this book, we focus on providing choice in all aspects of the learning process. When developing curriculum, one of the best ways to do this is to provide multiple avenues for students to demonstrate their understanding and skills. Instead of one test that assesses the class, provide a test, a paper, a project, and a conversation that all allow learners to share their knowledge in various ways.

3. KEEP THE CURRICULAR DOCUMENT EDITABLE.

This is a big one. When you are "finished" writing curriculum it can often be put aside as a paper document. Keep it online, digital, and open to edits throughout the year. Teachers need to share where they are changing, adding, and modifying on the fly for their learners. UDL allows this process to continue while still reaching for those goals shared with everyone.

Whether you are just getting started developing curriculum or revising an already written document, keep these principles in mind with a focus on universal design for learning. In doing so, you put the student's needs above everything else without compromising the goals and standards in the process.

·6·

ASSESSMENT

Performance Tasks over Tests

A big question many of us have in education is, Why are we still giving so many tests?

First, the obvious reason, because the state and other entities require us to give standardized tests each year. I think we can all agree this is the most pressing reason, and it has a trickle-down effect that we will get into later (i.e., the only way to get kids ready to take these tests is to give more tests). There is also a lot to unpack about why the state and other entities require us to give tests. While we get into it in this chapter, many others have broken down the political and financial reasons behind this phenomenon in greater detail.

Second, we must hold colleges and universities accountable. If they are still requiring tests like the SAT, ACT, and AP tests for admission, then we will inevitably be giving tests like those in our K–12 schools.

Third, there is a combination of things that are all interconnected: convenience, time, and data. Testing is the easiest, most time-efficient way to assess students' "understanding." And testing is the simplest way to get data on where students are compared to their peers (either locally, nationally, or internationally).

Fourth, because we've done it this way for a long time. I took tests and was measured by tests in school. Weren't you? Tests are written into our curriculum, they are baked into learning programs, and are typically tied to standards.

Of course, I don't think all testing is bad. There are often valid reasons for giving a test or a quiz, especially when we want to formatively see where students are at. Also, many tests are built with questions that are beyond surface-level regurgitation and hold real value.

Still, the research I'll share below (and many of our own experiences) tells us that testing is not the best or only way to share learning or demonstrate understanding. It has a major retention problem—sometimes 90 percent of knowledge that is correct on a test is lost after a few months. And finally, testing is not even the best way to prepare students to do well on those high-stakes standardized state tests, AP tests, and SAT and ACT tests.

If tests aren't the best way to assess, don't promote learning retention, and don't even prepare kids for the tests they "have" to take, then why are we still giving so many tests?

The follow-up question as to why are we still giving so many tests is, What can we do differently, and how do we pull it off?

I got the chance to talk with *Understanding by Design* author and curriculum and performance task expert Jay McTighe about all of these questions (and more). In an episode of *The Backwards Podcast*, we dove into driving factors of testing (curriculum, mandates, and more) and how performance tasks can, and should, be a replacement for many tests. We also got into the weeds about how we can replace tests at the local level, and what the future of the curriculum might look like.

IS PRACTICING THE TEST THE BEST WAY
TO PREPARE FOR A TEST?

As Jay McTighe said in *The Backwards Podcast*: "The logic of test prep is plausible and rooted in experience from other domains. For example, if you want to improve your performance in dribbling a basketball or piano playing, then you must practice those activities. Shouldn't the same apply to test taking?"[1]

I was a high school athlete and a football and lacrosse coach during my time as a middle-school and high-school English and language arts teacher. As a coach, I believed that winning was a byproduct (not just a goal) of the time, work, and focus the team displayed while practicing. Fundamentals, teamwork, strategy, tactics, planning, and execution all had a role in how well the team performed. But at least we had common goals.

In the classroom, we had varying goals. Each student was different. They all had unique interests, ideas, friends, and views on what success looked like to them in school.

My goals as a teacher were fairly simple. I wanted students to enjoy my class and find success in learning. I wanted to challenge students and give them an opportunity to grow. And I wanted to make sure their hard work in my class showed on the learning assessments that were measured.

I say this because, maybe, just like me, you only have one or two (or five) assessments each year that are actually measured beyond your classroom walls. And guess what? We care about what we are measured on. We focus on it, and we try to improve it. This is not only true for teachers; this impacts every person in any field.

A recent *Harvard Business Review* article talks about how the measures in other fields (business, medicine, science, etc.) have the exact same impact:

> It can't be that simple, you might argue—but psychologists and economists will tell you it is. Human beings

adjust behavior based on the metrics they're held against. Anything you measure will impel a person to optimize his score on that metric. What you measure is what you'll get. Period. This phenomenon plays out time and again in research studies.[2]

There is no way around it except to change what we measure. Or, to change the game entirely.

I was caught up in a circle of practice that was based on some misconceptions about how to improve the metric I was judged on as a teacher. It is important to note I was trying to do what was best for my students this entire time. I believe that almost all teachers have the best interests for their students and that their practice is predicated on preparing students in any way possible.

McTighe shares the misconceptions that led me down this test-prep trap as a young teacher; they are what many of us commonly believe are the reasons for preparing students for a test that we don't believe in. Here they are:

MISCONCEPTION #1: THE BEST (AND ONLY) WAY TO IMPROVE TEST SCORES IS TO PRACTICE THE TEST.

Here McTighe shares an analogy of the yearly physical exam with your doctor. Although the physician examines and measures your health, spending all your time trying to prepare for this physical by practicing the strategies would not make much sense.

"It would be thought silly to practice the physical exam as a way to improve one's health. But this confusion is precisely what we see in schools all over North America. Local educators, fearful of results, focus on the indicators, not their causes. The format of the test misleads us, in other words."[3]

MISCONCEPTION #2: STANDARDIZED TEST ITEMS INVOLVE PRIMARILY RECALL AND RECOGNITION, AND THUS DRILL AND PRACTICE WILL BE THE MOST EFFECTIVE METHOD TO PREPARE STUDENTS FOR THEM.

Grant Wiggins points out the flaw in this reasoning: "Even though the test format requires a selected response, it does not mean that the tested knowledge is necessarily simple. The [format] deceives you into thinking that since you are mimicking the format of the test, you are therefore mimicking the rigor of the test. But data show the opposite conclusively: local tests are often less rigorous than state and national tests even when they mimic the format."[4]

Too often, the information revealed by test-prep exercises identifies whether students have chosen the "correct" answer rather than helping teachers determine if they have a conceptual understanding of the underlying concepts and skills and if they can apply (transfer) those. "What Does It Mean to Learn" is an interesting talk about learning that unpacks this concept a bit more.[5]

It seems that testing students does not make them better test-takers, keep their retention, or improve their ability to achieve high scores on those state, AP, or SAT assessments.

HOW I GOT OUT OF THE TEST-PREP TRAP

It started small. First, I started to notice how disengaged my students were in class. Despite my efforts to use technology, create fun learning activities, and challenge my students, I was failing them in many ways. They cared more about getting a *grade* and playing the *game* of school than they did about learning. When I looked at the research it was clear that it was not just my class (and my students) that were showing signs of apathy.

On his website, Dangerously Irrelevant, Scott Mcleod shared results available from the annual Gallup poll of over 920,000 middle and high school students.[6] Here are a couple of key charts that Scott made from the data (remember this was pre-pandemic):

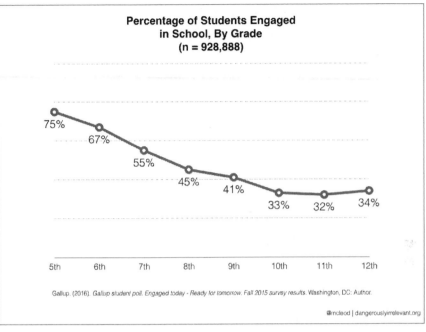

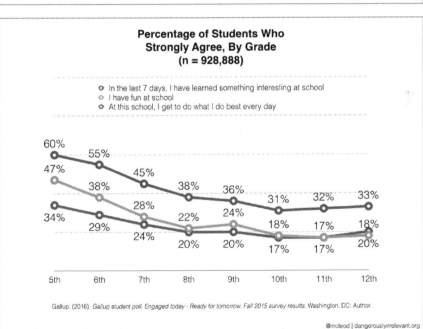

Interestingly enough, it seems that our students know this is happening. They know that they and their peers are often bored in school. We know that as teachers and administrators. What can we do about it?

WHAT DO WE DO INSTEAD OF TESTS?

The simple answer: performance tasks and a project-based learning (PBL) approach. Students are engaged more in these approaches, are able to demonstrate deeper levels of understanding, and are connected to real-world experiences and authentic tasks that are relevant and meaningful.[7]

Let's take a look at some of the research that supports making this shift. From a recent report on testing:

> A multi-year study of students taking AP United States Government and Politics (APGOV) and AP Environmental Sciences (APES) showed students did better on AP tests when engaging in project-based learning. APGOV students engaged in PBL in high-achieving schools "had a 30 percent higher pass rate on the APGOV exam than non-PBL students in comparable schools." The study was conducted from 2008 to 2013 and was led by the George Lucas Educational Foundation.
>
> That same study showed that APES students in poverty-impacted schools "had a 19 percent higher pass rate than non-PBL students in comparable schools matched nationally."[8]

Another study from researchers at the University of Michigan showed that second-grade students living in poverty increased their literacy and social studies skills through project-based learning. The study compared students at twenty high-poverty elementary schools. It showed "students whose teachers used the project-based learning curriculum made gains that were 63 percent higher than their peers in the control group in social studies and 23 percent higher in informational reading."[9]

WHAT ABOUT FAMILIES AND PARENTS? WHAT DO THEY WANT FROM AN EDUCATIONAL EXPERIENCE?

The Gallup report *Creativity in Learning* is based on a survey conducted in 2019 as a "nationally representative study" of teachers, students, and parents of students.[10] The focus was the extent to which "creativity in learning" is being fostered in American classrooms, what respondents think of it, and how technology supports it. Project-based learning is cited throughout the report.

Here are some highlights via PBLWorks:

> Teachers who often assign creative, project-based activities are more likely than other teachers to say their students display a range of learning and development goals, including building self-confidence, utilizing their unique strengths, and developing critical thinking and problem-solving skills.
>
> 68% percent of teachers say project-based assignments are a good measure of student learning, far more than the 12% who say the same about standardized tests.[11]

When parents and teachers were asked what they believe are the most important learning outcomes, the top three responses were:

1. "learning to think critically" (chosen by 64 percent of parents and teachers),
2. "problem-solving skills" (chosen by 51 percent of teachers; not asked of parents), and
3. "developing students' curiosity to learn beyond the classroom" (chosen by 36 percent of parents and 41 percent of teachers).[12]

Parents want their children to experience performance tasks and project-based learning. Take a look at this chart from the *Creativity in Learning* report that shows the percentage of parents who ranked the learning experiences as very important.

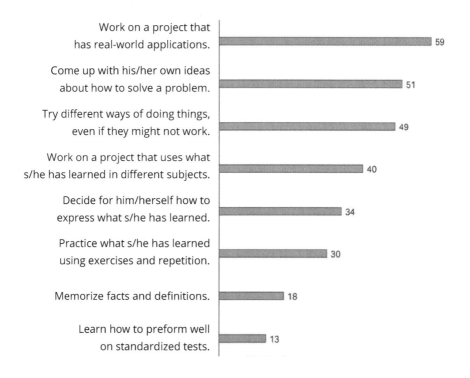

Work on a project that has real-world applications. — 59

Come up with his/her own ideas about how to solve a problem. — 51

Try different ways of doing things, even if they might not work. — 49

Work on a project that uses what s/he has learned in different subjects. — 40

Decide for him/herself how to express what s/he has learned. — 34

Practice what s/he has learned using exercises and repetition. — 30

Memorize facts and definitions. — 18

Learn how to preform well on standardized tests. — 13

Students want the kind of learning experiences that PBL delivers. Again, according to Gallup:

> Most students say they would like to spend more time on activities that give them input on their educational path, such as choosing what they learn in class and learning more about topics that most interest them.
>
> Two other activities a majority of students would like to spend more time on to help them see how what they are learning relates to real-life problems outside the classroom are 1) working on projects that can be used in

the real world, and 2) publishing or sharing projects with people outside their class or school.[13]

When Edutopia came out with an overview of the research around PBL, I nodded my head at the results.

Studies comparing learning outcomes for students taught via project-based learning versus traditional instruction show that when implemented well, PBL increases long-term retention of content, helps students perform as well as or better than traditional learners in high-stakes tests, improves problem-solving and collaboration skills, and improves students' attitudes towards learning (Strobel & van Barneveld, 2009; Walker & Leary, 2009). PBL can also provide an effective model for whole-school reform (National Clearinghouse for Comprehensive School Reform, 2004; Newmann & Wehlage, 1995).

A 2016 MDRC/Lucas Education Research literature review found that the design principles most commonly used in PBL align well with the goals of preparing students for deeper learning, higher-level thinking skills, and intra/ interpersonal skills (Condliffe et al., 2016).

No longer could the argument be about how well (or poorly) students would do on standardized assessments. The research was clear. When performance tasks and PBL were implemented well, students thrived in traditional tests and in a wide variety of soft-skills that are crucial to development and success beyond school.[14]

NOT ALL TESTS ARE CREATED EQUAL

Not all tests are created equal. Some tests are better than others and getting rid of all tests doesn't make that much sense—and it is most likely not possible in our current circumstances and environment. But, if we are currently giving tests as assessments 90 percent of the time, how can we shift that percentage down and provide more performance tasks as assessment options?

Creating curriculum is on my mind right now as I work with many schools struggling with these issues and with how they are impacting social-emotional learning and engagement with our students. It is also on my mind as a father of five who notices when they are excited about learning and wonders how we can do more of that across education.

The first half of this book has been developing the case for an adaptable curriculum. One that can withstand changes in and outside of education, but also one that works for the various learners in our schools. The second half of this book takes ideas and puts them into practice inside the learning environment. It builds on the research, strategies, and models shared while providing step-by-step ways to implement choice in the learning process.

If there was ever a time to build more student ownership, autonomy, and agency into the learning experience, that time is now.

PART 2

FLEXIBLE LEARNING EXPERIENCES

HOW DOES THIS APPLY TO OUR LEARNING EXPERIENCES AND STUDENTS?

When I look back on my best learning experiences, most of them came from outside the realm of traditional schooling when I was able to choose what I wanted to learn. The result? I was invested in the outcome of my learning process because the experience was centered around the types of learning I did best. They were all student-centered learning experiences, and I was the student.

There are many people calling for school reform, and they have many different types of agendas and plans on the table. But I believe the key is for schools to change in one single fundamental way: we need to let students choose as much of their learning path as possible.

Does this sound crazy? It's not. I have seen it work. That's why I wrote this book. This second part of the book identifies ten ways that any teacher can transform their classroom into a student-centered experience. Each chapter provides actionable steps to enable students to take charge of their learning path and be engaged and motivated by choice.

We will focus on real, actionable ways to let students choose their learning path in any school and how you as the teacher, instructional coach, or school leader can foster a flexible learning experience. The following chapters will focus on how a teacher can reach every student on his or her level and how to provide students a choice in:

- what they learn through content selection;
- how they learn through various forms of instruction and activities in the classroom;
- how they demonstrate their understanding and academic abilities through a variety of assessment formats;
- how communication is handled student to student, student to teacher, and school to home; and
- what types of technology they use and how they choose to present their learning.

All of this can happen in any school. You don't need to rip up the curriculum; you just need to think about it differently. This is the type of conversation we should be having in education because it is change that can happen and has happened already in many schools. So, let's start with a conversation and see what path it leads you down.

Your students will thank you.

· 7 ·

CONTENT

Choice in What We Learn

I spent a lot of time as a teacher figuring out new ways to inspire and motivate my students. Sometimes it worked, but often, I would fail to reach all of them. Then one day I gave my students choice. Not a "limited choice" assignment where they could pick one topic out of a box of topics, but *real* choice. You know what happened? Students were inspired and motivated to learn by themselves and with each other. And they did a much better job at inspiring than I ever could. Choice gives students the ability to go above and beyond our curricular limitations and allows them to innovate in ways we cannot predict.

That choice came in the form of the "20 Percent Project." They could learn whatever they wanted to learn in my class—with no real limitations—for 20 percent of our class time. It was extremely difficult for some students, and for others it was very natural. However, the real magic happened when the students began exploring and learning about their "choices" during class time.

As a teacher, I noticed some ways that choice impacted the learning process. Normally, we tell students what they are going to learn, give them resources and materials to learn (sometimes created by us; sometimes created by others), check for understanding, then provide feedback and help as needed.

This project was different because:

- students picked their learning topic and end goal,
- students predefined what they would consider a successful learning outcome, and
- in most cases I knew nothing about the topic they chose (e.g., if they chose to rebuild a car engine).

I was no longer the person with the most knowledge on the subject in the room, so I had to act fast and help in other ways. I would point them in the direction of strong research and mentoring opportunities. I would give feedback on their blogging and documenting. I would help in the learning process (I was learning as well) and give them a push toward some type of making, creating, or building aspect in their project.

THE IMPACT OF STUDENT CHOICE ON LEARNING

There were five specific ways student choice of content impacts the learning going on in my classroom:

1. CHOICE IMPROVES STUDENT BUY-IN.

In the beginning of the project, it was a challenge to get every student to actually choose a topic. Some wanted me to just give them a worksheet and tell them what they needed to do. However, once we got past this obstacle, the buy-in was already there. Students cared about what they were doing because they *chose* what they were doing. If they complained about their topic, I would let them switch to a new one so the buy-in would always remain the same.

2. CHOICE PUTS THE RESPONSIBILITY BACK IN THE STUDENTS' HANDS.

At the same time, the students knew that I was not the "expert" on their chosen topic. I didn't know much about learning sign language, so my responsibility as a teacher changed. Students could no longer come to me expecting an answer; they had to come to me for help in finding the answer. I was still the "lead learner" in my class, but I was learning alongside my students and not doing it for them. The responsibility for learning was firmly on their shoulders.

3. CHOICE ALLOWS FOR FLEXIBILITY.

If you've ever done a "passion project" (such as writing your own story or song), then you know that things change. The idea we initially start out with gets reworked and twisted into something completely new. Because I did not give requirements and deadlines with what they needed to complete, this project allowed for complete flexibility. Choice drove the students' actions and gave some room for lots of little (and sometimes big) changes along the way.

4. CHOICE EMBRACES CURRENT AND NEW PASSIONS.

To be honest, I didn't expect so many students to have no idea what they were interested in or passionate about. However, this project allowed students to find new passions and new interests—as well as embrace their current passions. This is important because they did not *need* to start with base knowledge—though sometimes they did. That meant for many students, they were just beginning to learn about a topic. For others, their topic was something they had been doing for many years. Choice put students on very different learning continuums during the project, but as we saw with the final presentations, this did nothing to limit the overall learning.

5. CHOICE LEADS TO GROWTH.

Ultimately, choice consistently led to growth (above and beyond what I expected). Because of the above factors, choice became a way for students to create their own learning path and assess how much they had learned. Almost every student came out of this project saying they had not only learned something new but also had been excited to grow through the process.

It was not always easy for my students (or for me as the teacher), but choice brought out the best in all of us as learners.

HOW TO BRING CONTENT CHOICE INTO YOUR CLASS AND GO BEYOND THE TEXTBOOK

There are certain subjects where content is fixed to the curriculum. In most math courses, you need to follow certain pathways to reach an understanding. In some science courses, the content is specific and you need to cover all of it by the end of the year. However, I've heard many teachers reference how they would like to move away from the "inch deep and mile wide" approach to curriculum.

If your content is specific, give your students choice to go deeper into a specific area of that content and become an "expert." If your curriculum is more skill-based, like a language arts class, the content can be ever changing. Students can master the same skills by reading various different pieces of content. They can understand grammar rules by more than just filling in worksheets. In classes and subjects where "skills" are the main goal (like many elementary classrooms) giving student choice in content empowers the students to be engaged with material that is both relevant and meaningful to them.

A STEP-BY-STEP GUIDE: CHOICE OF CONTENT IN THE CLASSROOM

To successfully allow for choice of content in your classroom, follow these seven steps (and modify as you see fit):

1. **Survey your class.** What are your students interested in? What are their passions? What do they do for fun? Find out

what makes each student tick and what they'll want to learn more about.

2. **Fit the choice to your curriculum.** Do you have curricular constraints that you can't break? If so, try and fit the choice to your content area. Can students go deeper into a specific topic they enjoy or are interested in? Are there offshoots to work you've already done in class? Can you use various content to hit specific skills like reading, writing, listening, and speaking? Make it work for your students and your class.

3. **Create a structure.** What time during the class, day, or week are you going to give students the opportunity to learn what they want to learn? Make sure to keep a specific structure in place so students know when to expect this and when to be prepared. It also helps to try it in short bursts before delving into a marking-period-long project.

4. **Start small.** If I had to go back and do it all over again, I would have started smaller. I would have given my students an opportunity to learn what they wanted to learn during one or two classes, then present on their learning. Then I would have gone into a bigger project or unit where they could choose larger goals for what they would learn, do, create, or make.

5. **Journal and reflect.** As students begin to learn their content, make sure they journal on the learning process. What are they learning? What is interesting? What ideas do they have? Reflect on what the process is like and why they are motivated to keep learning.

6. **Make something.** If all students do is learn, it can be tough to assess what they actually understand. One of the first changes I made to my project was to make sure students created something to present to their peers after the project was complete. This idea of a final product also helped to centralize what they were learning and give them an end goal for their work. As a

teacher, it helped me assess what types of learning the student did and where they could continue at a later point.

7. **Present.** After choosing a topic, researching, reading, watching, sharing, journaling, and making, the students need to present on their learning experience. Keep it short and simple. What did they learn? Why did they choose this topic, subject, or area? What did they make? What went well and what would they change?

Remember, the goal of giving students choice in the content they learn is twofold: First, it increases engagement and self-motivation because they choose the topic. As I often say to my students, "Only boring people are bored with this project!" Second, it allows students to learn important skills (and connect them to standards) that they'll need in your subject area and beyond—including research, presentation, and writing skills.

Start small and see what amazing things your students will accomplish!

SAMPLE PROJECT: A STANDARDS-BASED CHOICE ACTIVITY

GRADE LEVEL: 6–9

SUBJECT AREA: Writing (This can be used in writing across the curriculum.)

PURPOSE: Allow students to choose their learning topic, document their learning, and create a visual presentation to display their understanding.

COMMON CORE STATE STANDARDS:

CCSS.ELA-LITERACY.WHST.6-8.2.A
Introduce a topic clearly, previewing what is to follow; organize ideas, concepts, and information into broader categories as appropriate to

achieving purpose; include formatting (e.g., headings), graphics (e.g., charts, tables), and multimedia when useful to aiding comprehension.

CCSS.ELA-LITERACY.WHST.6–8.5

With some guidance and support from peers and adults, develop and strengthen writing as needed by planning, revising, editing, rewriting, or trying a new approach, focusing on how well purpose and audience have been addressed.

CCSS.ELA-LITERACY.WHST.6–8.6

Use technology, including the internet, to produce and publish writing and present the relationships between information and ideas clearly and efficiently.

CCSS.ELA-LITERACY.WHST.6–8.7

Conduct short research projects to answer a question (including a self-generated question), drawing on several sources and generating additional related, focused questions that allow for multiple avenues of exploration.

TIME: 180 minutes

STRUCTURE/TIMELINE:

1. Introduce the project to students as a way for them to learn what they are interested about (that you've already covered this year) or something they've always wanted to learn. Hand out a project overview, goal-setting sheet, and requirements. (15 mins.)
2. Have students fill out an "interest final four" where they pit their top four interests or passions against each other and choose a final winner to work on for the project. (10 mins.)
3. Have students answer three questions about their topic of interest. (10 mins.)

    a. What do you want to learn about this topic?

    b. Why does it interest you so much?

    c. How are you going to display what you have learned?

4. Provide time to research and document. (60 mins.)

    a. Have students research their topic using the internet, school library, and other online resources.

    b. Students should document what resources they have read or watched, and what they learned about their topic from those resources (use a double-entry journal).

    c. Students can document their learning in a notebook or online via a blogging platform.

    d. Repeat steps *a–c*.

5. Have students share with a small group. (20 mins.)

    a. In groups, students can share what they have learned about their topic, where they've learned it from, and what else they want to learn before creating a presentation.

    b. Keep this structured to two minutes of sharing, then two minutes of feedback from the group. It's short and to the point.

6. Provide time for final research and learning. (30 mins.)

    a. Go back and repeat the earlier steps for learning with a renewed focus on areas of interest brought up in the feedback from small groups.

7. Have students create a presentation. (30 mins.)

    a. Choose a presentation tool. This can be multimedia or a live display.

    b. Create a presentation with the following pieces:

        i. The chosen topic

        ii. Why the topic was chosen

        iii. What resources were used to learn

        iv. What was learned along the way

        i. Three takeaways from the learning

        v. What the student would do differently

           vi. How others in class can get started learning about this topic if interested

    c. Practice the presentation.

8. Have students present. (20 mins.)

    a. For time purposes, either have students upload presentations online so they can watch regardless of class time, or create a gallery walk.

    b. For a gallery walk, have half of the class present for the first ten minutes and have students walk to topics that interest them. The second half of class will present during the last ten minutes.

9. Allow time for a final reflection. (5–10 mins.)

·8·

INSTRUCTION

Flexibility in How We Learn

Take a moment and think about your favorite learning experience ever. What did you enjoy about it? Why did you get so much out of this experience compared to the thousands of other learning experiences you've had over the years? Chances are you had a great teacher, a safe environment for learning, and something special that put this experience over the top.

As teachers, we want every student to have their best learning experience with us in our classrooms, yet our problem is that we often try to find the "something special" that will be the same for all of our students. That's probably not going to happen. Students (just like teachers and anyone else) learn differently. Some enjoy group work; others prefer to work alone. Some understand better through auditory learning, while others understand better through visual learning. The list of learning differences in students goes on and on. As humans we each have specific sets of circumstances that allow us to learn best. This set of circumstances changes over time, and although it is fluid, a teacher does not have much control over what is going to allow a student to learn best that day. Unless we give choice.

One of the basic tenets of differentiated instruction is it allows a teacher to reach many students at different levels of understanding. By differentiating what we teach, and how we teach it, we are able to reach the entire classroom instead of the small group of students who are going to follow along with direct instruction.

Let's take this a step further and understand one important belief about instruction: We are no longer the gatekeepers of knowledge. But we are experts at how to learn. The gatekeeper method has teachers in the front of the classroom or lecture hall or computer screen talking about what they know and explaining how they came to that understanding. Often, we tweak the gatekeeper method by "spicing up" the lesson with technology or other fun activities. But, if the teacher (or textbook) is still the one holding all of the knowledge, it won't matter what types of activities you do, students will not feel they own the learning. This is a key understanding because, as teachers, we have the ability to teach the same skill one hundred different ways. Yet we often choose to teach the skill in one way. Maybe two ways. And, if we are truly on top of our game, three ways.

When we differentiate, we build the choices into our instruction and, conversely, the learning process. *That's a lot of work for the teacher.* It can be a lot of planning when we differentiate instruction. But what is our main goal for any learning activity?

Most would say our goal should be to have students demonstrate understanding of the concept or skill covered in the learning activity. Instead, I'd argue that goals should be tied to the assessment and should be seen as *separate* from the actual learning activity.

For any learning activity our goal should be *engagement.* Why engagement? Because student engagement predicts success better than any other metric in the classroom.

ENGAGEMENT VERSUS COMPLIANCE

We know the best learning experiences happen when the learner's attitude, attention, and commitment to the process is at an all-time high. This combination is what Phil Shlechty calls "engagement" in his fantastic levels:

ENGAGEMENT

- The student sees the activity as personally meaningful.
- The student's level of interest is sufficiently high that he persists in the face of difficulty.
- The student finds the task sufficiently challenging that she believes she will accomplish something of worth by doing it.
- The student's emphasis is on optimum performance and on "getting it right."

STRATEGIC COMPLIANCE

- The official reason for the work is not the reason the student does the work—she substitutes her own goals for the goals of the work.
- The substituted goals are instrumental—grades, class rank, college acceptance, parental approval.
- The focus is on what it takes to get the desired personal outcome rather than on the nature of the task itself—satisfactions are extrinsic.
- If the task doesn't promise to meet the extrinsic goal, the student will abandon it.

RITUAL COMPLIANCE

- The work has no meaning to the student and is not connected to what does have meaning.
- There are no substitute goals for the student.

- The student seeks to avoid either confrontation or approbation.
- The emphasis is on minimums and exit requirements—what do I have to do to get this over and get out?

RETREATISM

- The student is disengaged from current classroom activities and goals.
- The student is thinking about other things or is emotionally withdrawn from the action.
- The student rejects both the official goals and the official means of achieving the goals.
- The student feels unable to do what is being asked or is uncertain about what is being asked.
- The student sees little that is relevant to life in the academic work.

REBELLION

- The student is disengaged from current classroom activities and goals.
- The student is actively engaged in another agenda.
- The student creates her own means and her own goals.
- The student's rebellion is usually seen in acting out—and often in encouraging others to rebel.[1]

The issue with engagement is that many of us were taught that a classroom should look like the strategic compliance level. This is the "well-managed" classroom that many teachers strive to replicate on a daily basis, and the type of classroom that is often praised in classroom observations by administrators around the world. I spent many years trying to "manage" a classroom instead of engaging learners.

When you first walk into a classroom that is loud and has kids all over the room (some in partners, some in groups, and some alone) using different learning tools, your first thought may not be engagement. If you're not sure what engagement looks like, begin asking these questions:

- What type of attitude does the student have toward the learning activity? What is the evidence?
- What level of attention does the student have toward the learning activity? What is the evidence?
- What level of commitment does the student have toward the learning activity? What is the evidence?

When you ask these three questions, as a teacher or administrator, the answers will lead you to an understanding of student engagement, compliance, or withdrawal.

HOW CHOICE IMPACTS STUDENT ENGAGEMENT AND INSTRUCTION

In chapter 7, we looked at ways to learn the same skill through students' choice of content. In this chapter, we are flipping that a bit. The reality of most schools is that certain content must be taught. Our goal is to figure out how to teach the same content while giving the students a choice of instructional experiences.

The key to this approach is getting all students engaged. That means all students must have high attention and high commitment. One of the best and most manageable ways to do this is through in-class stations.

As a teacher, I used the station model a lot, and I really believe it has the power to keep students engaged, moving, and working through different types of content. However, when I asked my students about stations (especially at the high-school level) I sometimes received feedback that they didn't like them. Why?

Well, many students said that they only liked a few of the stations and some of the other stations were boring to them. Interestingly, the stations they liked and the stations they thought were boring varied widely depending on the student and class.

I had my aha moment about stations during a fall football practice. As a coach you want to make sure the players are not only engaged but also focusing on skills that pertain to their position and role on the team. During the station part of our practice, the quarterback and receivers went to one station, the lineman to another station, and the running backs to a different station.

I thought, *Why can't I do this in class?*

The difference would be allowing students to choose which stations they wanted to participate in and giving them an opportunity to go deep with the content based on their preferred instructional activity. When I brought this idea back into the classroom, my students were excited. They now had the power to choose, and from that choice came a level of ownership previously missing in station activities.

THE PICK-YOUR-STATION ACTIVITY EXAMPLE

First, you start with the content or unit that is built into the curriculum. In this case let's use photosynthesis as our example.

Next, you have to decide what instructional resources and methods you are going to use to deliver this content. Some examples of this are:

- Direct instruction for the full class (virtual or in person)
- Direct instruction for a small group (virtual or in person)
- Direct instruction in a conference
- Read material in a textbook
- Read material in articles
- Listen to material (podcast or audiobooks)
- View material (possibly flip the lesson with a video)
- Listen, view, and read material (an interactive presentation with audio)
- Online simulation of photosynthesis

Traditionally, we'll choose one or two of these methods and create a lesson plan or activity based on what we believe is the best way to teach this topic or content. Sometimes, as discussed earlier, we'll take four or five of these methods and create a station activity.

Here, you can pick five or six activities and let your students choose two or three that truly pique their interest. If you remember from chapter 5 on UDL (universal design for learning), this is the essence of what Katie Novak calls "a buffet of learning"—instead of being a short order cook and reacting to students' needs as they arise.

It is important to note that there must be an assessment of some type that you are working toward. In this case, we'll use a photosynthesis lab as our final project-based assessment. For students to successfully complete the lab and analyze the results, they'll have to understand:

- What photosynthesis is and why it is important
- What the process looks like
- Key terms and vocabulary for the content
- How this connects to other units in science that you've covered

The Pick-Your-Station activity provides this information in a variety of formats and experiences. As students choose the station, you'll get a better grasp on what types of activities work for them and which ones they find engaging.

Throughout the stations, students should be recording what they are learning and what they understand through a guided set of notes. The result is that all students should be prepared to successfully complete the photosynthesis lab activity.

In a traditional classroom setting, students may not be engaged through a presentation or connect to the instructional delivery method. Here, they have the choice to go with what works best for them as a learner. This is flexibility in action.

A STEP-BY-STEP GUIDE FOR YOUR CLASSROOM: PICK-YOUR-STATION

1. Identify a unit, concept, or skill and what you want students to know, do, or make in order to demonstrate their understanding and proficiency.

2. Create or choose an assessment that allows students to demonstrate mastery.

3. List various instructional methods, resources, and strategies to prepare students for the assessment.

4. Choose four to six instructional methods to turn into station activities. Each station activity should be a similar length in time and cover common material. Here is where you can add different types of technology or hands-on experiences to the learning process.

5. Create a workflow at each station for the students to follow. Have notes and formative checks as part of the station-design process. Allow for reflection at each station when planning how long students will have to complete the activity.

6. Introduce the different stations to students and describe what the goals of the activity are as well as the assessment this is leading up to.

7. Let students pick two or three stations based on their interests.

8. Start the timer and keep rotations from station to station even. A few of the stations might need more guidance than others. Make sure you aren't just "managing" this activity but instead, truly act as a guide and expert learner at various stations.

9. Once the station rotations are complete, put students into small groups to "jigsaw" the reflection. Bring students from different stations together to reflect on and share their learning experience.

10. Listen to reflections and check the formative pieces for each station to see if every student is prepared for the assessment.

If not, feel free to go through one more station together as a class or talk about any topics or concepts they did not understand during the activity.

11. Give the assessment (see chapter 9 for more on this).

As you can see, the process may take a little more time on the front end from the teacher, but you'll know that students are prepared for an assessment by going through this activity.

When I began using technology in the classroom, these activities also turned into online experiences that could be done at any time. My ultimate goal as a teacher was to see my students succeeding and demonstrating understanding of concepts and skills at a high level. The simple act of giving the students choice changed how my students viewed our assessments and how they prepared for assessments.

·9·

UNDERSTANDING

Flexible Formative Assessment

My first full year of teaching was as an eighth-grade language arts teacher. It was my dream job at the time. I loved the energy of middle-school students, and I was still taller than most of them.

What made my job even better than expected was our teaching schedule. Because our middle-school teams had two language arts teachers, I taught three eighty-five-minute blocks instead of five forty-minute blocks. Although this schedule meant more time teaching, there were fewer students per class and fewer students for my entire course load. It helped in grading especially (think of how long it takes to grade 130 papers versus sixty-five papers).

An added benefit that I did not see when I started the school year was how much extra time it gave me to understand and get to know my students. When you spend eighty minutes a day for 180 days with someone, you really get to know them. I think of the connections elementary teachers can make with their students and know their bond is even stronger.

Midway through the school year, one of my students asked me if I'd share some of my own writing with them. I actually couldn't believe I had not done this yet. I had shared some examples of papers that I crafted, but although these were original, they weren't connected to the type of learning that I often did outside of school. I told them I'd read something I wrote the next day. Oddly, although we did a lot of fun activities, it seemed like my students were more excited than they ever had been before.

That night I took out a memoir-type piece I had recently written about a friend passing away and how it changed my outlook on life. I wondered if this was "too heavy" for my eighth-grade students, and then I remembered that we all deal with loss and hopefully this could show how I grew since this tough time.

As I read aloud the memoir, *Three Bands on My Wrist*, to my students, they sat and listened quietly. There was no technology involved. There was no particular instructional strategy being employed. It was just me, my words, and their attention. After I finished, they wanted to write their own memoirs, and we began that same class period.

I can honestly say that some of their writing that week was the most inspired I have seen in all my years of teaching. And it was their choice. The next year, I moved up to the high-school English department, and two years later, I was teaching tenth-grade English to many of the exact same students I had in eighth grade.

When they came into class, I already knew each student—I knew their backgrounds, family situations, interests, and learning tendencies. I was a bit more challenging as a tenth-grade teacher and that ruffled some feathers early on, but after that, we were able to do some high-level types of activities because relationships were already built.

However, I did have one problem. Although I knew them personally, I wasn't able to see how much they had grown as writers over the past year. I had kept a few papers from that eighth-grade year, but not one for every student. When I asked the ninth-grade teachers if they had saved any of their papers, the answer was no. There was no student work to look at.

This was another light bulb moment for me as a teacher. Because we usually start fresh with students we have never taught before, we tend to want to make our own judgments on their abilities from the first few assignments and assessments. It's on those first glances that we base our opinions and pedagogical strategies for our students.

Yet, I had taught this group a year and a half ago. I knew them and what they could do, but I still wasn't able to see how much they had grown in the past year. That is when we made the decision to start digital portfolios. I highly recommend doing this, not only for teachers but for entire departments and schools. It adds true choice to the assessment process. Here's why.

WHAT CAN STUDENTS DO? THE PORTFOLIO JOURNEY

We always want to know what our students understand and are able to do and apply. The problem is that a multiple-choice assessment rarely provides that information. But they are used because they are easy to grade, easy to distribute, and easy to reuse year after year with various updates. It is why many standardized assessments are multiple-choice and why the SAT and ACT use this model for most of their questions.

Not only do multiple choice assessments not provide the best information about students' abilities but what's even worse is that the idea of "data-driven" instruction is based on these various multiple-choice assessments and what they say about our students' abilities.

What kind of learning do these assessments promote?

- Regurgitation and memorizing facts from study guides or stories
- An "only one right answer" mentality
- Smart guessing and "playing the game"
- The idea that answers have to already be in your head

The list could go on. As a former teacher who gave multiple-choice tests and as an SAT tutor who taught students how to take these tests, I'm embarrassed to say I also once tied rigorous and tough multiple-choice questions to deep learning.

But when I had that group of eighth-grade students again in tenth grade, I saw firsthand what kind of information I can get from different forms of assessments. I was able to see how they did on standardized and district-level assessments. But unless their scores were off the charts (high or low), it didn't give me much information on what kind of learner they were or what kind of work they could produce. What I can see by looking at students' work is much different. A student portfolio shows me the following:

- What the assignment, activity, or assessment was and how the student approached it
- What kinds of personal experiences and biases they brought to the assignment
- How well they demonstrated an understanding of the content
- How well they demonstrated their skill ability
- Usually, some kind of reflection or metacognitive piece on what they did
- If they improved or not with the next piece in the portfolio

This is not only what every teacher wants to see from their former students but it also makes it much easier to assess the growth of a student over the course of a semester or full year compared to how much a final test or culminating project would show.

Portfolios helped me to see where my students were struggling and where they were exceeding my expectations. Portfolios also allowed for student choice in the assessment process, which, as we know, leads to student engagement and ownership of their learning.

CHOICE IN DEMONSTRATING ABILITY AND UNDERSTANDING

Because we love multiple choice so much, let's take a quick quiz. A student is trying to demonstrate their understanding on the rise and fall of Napoleon. In order to show what they know about this historic time period and the reasons behind Napoleon's rise and fall, students can be assessed through which activity (circle all that apply):

1. Writing a five-paragraph essay on the rise and fall of Napoleon
2. Creating an infographic on the rise and fall of Napoleon
3. Creating a political cartoon and rationale on the rise and fall of Napoleon
4. Creating a five-minute minidocumentary on the rise and fall of Napoleon
5. Creating a fictional, serial-like podcast of interviews with key players in Napoleon's life
6. All of the above

Don't you just love the "all of the above" option? In any one of these options, you could assess a student's understanding of the topic or situation and their ability to demonstrate the appropriate skill. What's different about this scenario is the choice provided to students allows them to engage in the material and claim some ownership over the assessment activity.

A STEP-BY-STEP PROCESS TO CREATING CHOICE-BASED ASSESSMENTS

We've already discussed in chapter 2 the understanding by design framework from *Understanding by Design* by Grant Wiggins and Jay McTighe. Let's use their concept of the backward-design process to create a template for how to put together a learning unit.

We want to create the assessment first, and then backward design the unit so that the content and activities students are doing match the skills and standards covered on the assessments. For our purposes this is extremely important.

1. CHOOSE YOUR UNIT.

This is most likely decided by your current curriculum.

2. CHOOSE SKILLS AND STANDARDS.

In this step you will choose the skills you want your students to master and the applicable standards for the content and skills you are covering. Hopefully this is also somewhat covered by your current curriculum.

For example, let's say the unit is all about historical figures in your state or area. You have a set curriculum and text to read (often an informational text such as a textbook). This current example can be for fifth grade. Jump onto the standards website (www.corestandards.org) and search for applicable standards for fifth grade "Reading: Informational Text" to find this:

CCSS.ELA-LITERACY.RI.5.1

Quote accurately from a text when explaining what the text says explicitly and when drawing inferences from the text.

CCSS.ELA-LITERACY.RI.5.2

Determine two or more main ideas of a text and explain how they are supported by key details; summarize the text.

CCSS.ELA-LITERACY.RI.5.3

Explain the relationships or interactions between two or more individuals, events, ideas, or concepts in a historical, scientific, or technical text based on specific information in the text.

3. CREATE ASSESSMENTS.

Now you will put the pieces together for various assessments. The assessment must focus on similar content (historical figures), similar skills and standards (we will hit on the three standards mentioned earlier), and have a similar rubric for grading.

Let's talk about the rubric for a moment. Here's where many teachers get stuck, because creating a grading rubric takes a lot of time. And who has that much time? Lucky for all of us, there are some very easy and efficient ways to create standards-based rubrics online. My favorite tool is RubiStar (http://rubistar.4teachers.org). It took me less than five minutes to create this sample rubric based on our example standards:

Example Common Core Rubric (LBC)
Common Core-aligned rubric (5th Grade)

	Below 5th (weakest)	Beginning	Emerging	Proficient	Above 5th (strongest)
Quote text in Explanations (¶) Paragraph-level Reading: Informational Text: RI.5.1					
Quote text in Inferences Sentence-level Reading: Informational Text: RI.5.1					
Determine Main Idea (¶) Paragraph-level Reading: Informational Text: RI.5.2					
Key Detail Support Whole document Reading: Informational Text: RI.5.2					
Summarize Text Whole document Reading: Informational Text: RI.5.2					
Explain Relationships or Interactions (¶) Paragraph-level Reading: Informational Text: RI.5.3					

What's nice about RubiStar is the ability to personalize and change all of the categories in the top row. The categories down the side are straight from the standards and skills we pulled for this unit.

Ask yourself after creating the rubric, "Can this work for various types of assessments for this unit?" If the answer is yes, then you've got a rubric to work with. If the answer is still no, you'll either have to create a new rubric or revisit step two for some clarity.

4. PROVIDE STUDENTS A CHOICE FOR THEIR ASSESSMENT.

Step four is allowing your students to choose their preferred assessment or create their own assessment. As we discussed in the previous chapter with the pick-your-station activity, choice empowers students and engages them in the material.

I used to have a bank of various assessment types that my students could look through and choose the assessment that best fit their personality, interests, and learning styles. However, over time more and more students started to use the first option on that list: make your own assessment. Some of the assessment ideas that came from students include:

- "I want to make a *Saturday Night Live* parody skit around this topic and poke fun at the way it was handled in a historical sense."
- "I want to conduct an in-depth interview with the author, where my friend will play the role of the author, and we'll get into a heated argument."
- "I want to create a flip-book style comic to show the character's story arc."

This list could go on. Students are much more creative in their assessment ideas than I ever could be!

5. CONFERENCE WITH STUDENTS ABOUT THEIR PLAN.

You'll want to make sure students understand the following:

- What the end-goal is for this assessment
- How they are being assessed (look at the rubric together)
- What the expectations are for their work
- What a timeline looks like for their assessment
- An action plan of how they are going to get it finished

This is one of the most important pieces of allowing choice in assessment. A traditional assessment dictates all of the terms listed above. You know when the test date is, what type of content is going to be on the test, how much each question is worth, and when the study guide needs to be completed. But here, the short conference serves as a guiding plan for completing the choice-based assessment and demonstrating a high level of understanding.

My students always felt better after this miniconference because the goals, outcomes, steps, and how they would be ultimately assessed on their project were clearly laid out in front of them.

6. DIGITIZE AND SHARE THE PROJECT.

In this step, you digitize and share the project with the class and in the student's portfolio. Regardless of what assessment type students choose, they need to create a digital record of this assessment to put in their online portfolio. This is easy to do if the work was done on a digital device, but if it was not, you'll need to take pictures (or video recordings) to upload to the portfolio.

Teachers ask me all the time what they should use for student digital portfolios. I'd first recommend using a platform that your school is already using (Google Apps for Education, Microsoft 365, or Apple options). By starting out with a simple Google Drive (or SkyDrive) folder, you can eventually give the students a choice down the road of what platform they want to create their digital portfolio on so they can share it with the world. Here is where students will make their own websites using WordPress, Weebly, Wix, Squarespace, and many more options.

7. GRADE THE ASSESSMENT.

The assessment will get both a teacher grade and a student grade. A big piece of this type of assessment is to have students grade themselves using the rubric. They were fully aware (from the earlier conference) of what was expected and how their work should demonstrate understanding. The act of reflecting and grading themselves makes this all the more transparent.

After students grade themselves, I would look at the rubric and their assessment to see if I had different thoughts on what was demonstrated. Interestingly, most of my students were incredibly honest throughout this process and were harder on themselves than I might have been when grading them.

If the student's grade and my grade were completely off base, then I would have another short conference to talk about expectations and outcomes for this assessment so we could get on the same page.

8. ASSESS THE PORTFOLIO.

At the end of the unit, marking period, semester, or year, it's important to assess the overall work of the student through their portfolio. Art teachers have been doing this for years, and more and more colleges are requesting to see real student work as part of the admission process.

To make a real-world connection, think of your students' digital portfolios as the first steps in their academic resume and also in crafting their personal brand and professional identity. The choices they make in what they create, make, or do for assessments will directly impact the choices they make in their career and life path. If they do not document this journey, then it will be hard to reflect on why they made choices and what they have learned along the way.

·10·

FLIPPED

A Simple Approach to Adaptable Learning

When Khan Academy burst onto the scene, my initial reaction was to laugh. What was so special about it? Khan Academy touted its site as an online learning platform with videos on almost every subject. Khan Academy let teachers "flip their instruction" by presenting the lesson or lecture at home through video and working on what would have been homework in school with the teacher.

The more and more I thought about Khan Academy and the idea of "flipping your classroom," the more I became frustrated with the general public's perception of teaching and learning. If the media and public believed that watching videos at home the night before school was a solution to all of our educational problems, then what was the point of teaching at all? I was annoyed, a bit angry, and generally confused at how this platform could be seen as such a savior.

In the midst of my frustration, I went to look at what others were saying about Khan Academy and the idea of "flipping the classroom" with video. I was an English teacher at the time, and it didn't make sense to me. We had always sent the content home in the form of reading and done the work in class in the form of conversations, formative assessments, Socratic seminars, and analysis.

Investigating the Khan Academy learning method led me to another aha moment. I realized that I didn't really know what teaching looked like in other subjects besides my own. Like many teachers, I was so wrapped up in my own content area that I forgot that students went to six other classes a day in our high school.

Two years after this epiphany, I left the classroom for a new role as a K–12 technology staff developer. I was tasked with helping to integrate technology into the classroom and run our one-to-one laptop initiative at the high school. My new job was something I always wanted to do. I loved working with my colleagues, and I was especially passionate about the transformative role technology can play in the learning process.

That year I grew more as a teacher than any other time in my career for one reason: I watched other teachers teach.

I helped teachers plan, watched them teach, talked about their subject areas or their grade levels (in elementary school), and reflected on what worked well and what could be improved. Although my focus was on technology, the real discussions happened around instructional strategies, pedagogy, and best or next practices.

After a year, I better understood what the entire scope of an educational experience looked like. I had previously held assumptions about subjects like science, math, and social studies from my own middle- and high-school experiences as a student. Sure, I had cross-curricular conversations over the years with my colleagues in these areas, but never before had I seen what it took to plan and execute a lesson, activity, or assessment in their subject areas.

Without a doubt I was most blown away by the math teachers in our school. Students came into their classrooms with a preconceived notion about whether they were good or bad at math. Most of the math skills built upon each other, so if students had previously struggled and "just got by" the year before, they would come in behind, possibly fall further behind, and struggle again throughout the school year. It was a snowball effect—and the snowball got bigger and bigger each year.

Math classes were also where I saw some of the biggest need to differentiate. Students were on various levels of understanding for all kinds of concepts. There was no possible way you could "teach to the middle" and actually help the students who were struggling or challenge the students who had already mastered the concept or skill. Teaching "to the middle" left two-thirds of the class with ineffective instruction, and the teachers I worked with knew this struggle all too well.

I was planning with a third-year math teacher who caught me off guard when she said, "I'm constantly checking to see if they understand what we are doing, but when 80 percent of the class gets it, that means five of my students are falling behind when we move forward. Not only that, but another five to ten students understand the material so well, they could possibly teach most of it to themselves at the pace we are going."

I thought, *There has to be a better way.*

That's when I went back to the idea of Khan Academy. Instructional video lessons were a possible solution to this problem that was most likely repeated in schools across the country and world. The videos could serve as remediation or to push some students who worked at a quicker pace further ahead with that concept. In theory, the idea was great. But, like many good ideas, in practice it didn't work too well. Students had to want to watch the video—just like any homework— and students had to understand the instruction in the video for it to work. The problem was that sometimes it was not high-quality instruction, and there were no teachers to answer questions while the video was playing.

When we discussed the idea of "flipping the classroom" in our math classes, we wanted to focus on how it could help teachers differentiate instead of just sending home instruction for homework. What came out of this discussion and planning was an amazingly simple and effective way to differentiate and provide some structured choice in the learning process. It was both simple for the students to understand and effective in how students could move from a low level of understanding to a high level of understanding. And it was an engagement boost!

The difficult piece was designing the lessons and activities in order for this type of differentiated flipped model to work successfully. Luckily, we had some amazing teachers who worked incredibly hard to develop this model. Let's break it down.

THE THREE-TIERED FLIPPED MODEL FOR INSTRUCTION

As we walk through these ten steps to "flip" your instruction and set up a working model of differentiation in your class, keep in mind a few things.

First, realize that this can work in any subject area. In order for it to work successfully, a teacher must come up with clear objectives on what students need to know, and how they will demonstrate that knowledge. You'll also have to be able to teach the main concept through video, and students will need a way to access that video at home.

Second, don't spend too much time thinking about the resources you use to make the video. I'll share some that work really well in the final part of this chapter, but often teachers get stuck in the technical side of things instead of just making it and getting better with production over time.

Third, make sure you use this strategy to find out what your students know and what they are missing, then get them to a place where they can demonstrate that understanding. Differentiation may sound difficult, but really it is providing various pathways for students to achieve the same level of success. When you pre-assess students, the goal is not to see who did the homework, but instead how your instruction can meet students where they are in their current level of understanding.

A STEP-BY-STEP GUIDE: CHOICE IN DIFFERENTIATION

Here are ten steps (some are longer than others) to get this model working with your class:

1. Teachers identify a particular concept or skill to focus their instruction. This is often dictated by your curriculum.

2. Teachers create a short video screencast (using Screencast-o-matic.com) walking students through the concept, explaining the reasoning and steps, and providing examples of the skill in action.

3. Teachers edit and upload the video to YouTube or Vimeo.

4. Students watch the video the night or day before class and take notes or answer some quick comprehension questions.

5. When students arrive at class the following day, the teacher hands out (or gives digitally) a short five-question pre-assessment based on the video and instruction from the night before.

6. Students answer the questions to the best of their abilities and then score a partner's assessment (or self-score their own).

   a. Students end up in three tiers based on the pre-assessment score. The goal for all students is to end up in tier C by the end of class.

      i. Score a 0–1 and you are in tier A.

      ii. Score a 2–3 and you are in tier B.

      iii. Score a 4–5 and you are in tier C.

7. For the first third of class:

   a. Tier A sits down and re-watches the video from the night before with a teacher-created handout with new questions.

   b. The teacher gets tier B into groups (or partners) to work on refining some of the skills and concepts together. They can use the video as a guide and call on the teacher to help during their group work.

    c. Tier C is given a higher-level application challenge.

8. For the second third of class:

    a. The teacher heads over to tier A after the video is complete to answer any questions they might have on the concept and give the entire group some questions to answer. The students answer questions individually, then they move on to tier B.

    b. Tier B takes another short formative assessment (individually) to show their understanding after the group-work on the concept. Those that score a 4–5 move onto tier C.

    c. Tier C continues to work on the challenge. If they have completed it, they begin to help new students coming into their group.

9. For the last third of class:

    a. Tier B students work in partners or groups and take the next formative assessment when they are ready. The teacher floats between tier B and tier C helping and challenging as needed. Tier B students are helped by classmates and the teacher to move to tier C before the end of the class.

    b. Tier C students finish the challenge and work to create a challenge for the following class (or next year's class).

A RECAP OF THE GOALS ACHIEVED THROUGH THESE TEN STEPS

First, you start with some type of work at home or in the beginning of class. Then you quickly assess each student's base knowledge of that concept. The pre-assessment separates your class into three tiers of understanding. The goal is to move students through tiers and provide different levels of support, with all students landing at the final tier for a challenge activity by the end of class.

The key to making this successful is to embed choices into the activities during class. Allow students to pick partners and groups. Give students multiple types of questions to answer and activities to complete. Give the second tier options on how they are assessed before moving to the final tier. Provide the final tier with options and a choice to challenge their understanding and move past the application to a higher-level of thinking.

I would recommend starting with a concept or skill that some students typically master more quickly than others. In this case, you will have already experienced the frustration of having students at all different levels of understanding and know that there has to be a better way to instruct the entire class.

Start small with a short video and quick activities at each of the levels. That way, when you move to bigger units of study, students will be familiar with the process and expectations. It's amazing to watch the negative "snowball" effect of students falling behind stop immediately. In this model there is no "falling too far behind," because students are all expected to reach a certain level of mastery by the end of the class. Choice and formative feedback are the fuel that gets them there!

·11·

COMMUNICATION

Connecting with Folks in Ways That Work for Them

In 1936, Dale Carnegie wrote a book called *How to Win Friends and Influence People*. It went on to sell over thirty million copies. It still sells today and is probably one of the best books on how to improve your social skills.

In his little book, there are so many big quotes and lessons on how to actually "get along" with people and have some influence. As leaders and teachers, this is a great book to learn from. We are constantly striving to have a positive impact and influence on teachers and students—yet we often put that "skill" on the back burner. Instead, we focus on debating the Common Core, talking about the next big thing in "Ed Tech," and looking at how many different ways we can "reform" education. Maybe some things do need to change (I'm sure we can all agree on that broad statement), but our focus has to stay on positively impacting the lives of students in our school.

THE REAL INFLUENCE WE HAVE ON STUDENTS

In the *Journal of Student Engagement* Lauren Liberante writes:

> The teacher-student relationship is one of the most pow-
> erful elements within the learning environment. A major
> factor affecting students' development, school engagement
> and academic motivation, teacher-student relationships
> form the basis of the social context in which learning
> takes place (Hughes & Chen, 2011; Roorda et al.).
>
> Teacher–student interactions are not only influenced
> by a number of aspects including gender, but in turn also
> influence a student's academic outcomes and behavior.
> Supportive and positive relationships between teach-
> ers and students ultimately promote a "sense of school
> belonging" and encourage students to "participate coop-
> eratively in classroom activities" (see Hughes & Chen,
> 2011, p.278).[1]

Liberante's research makes the case that the relationships in our
education system may prove to be the most effective way to improve
student engagement. All of us that teach and work with children
understand the importance of relationships. We know that spending
time helping a student one-on-one does more than a small group setting. Yet, we often forget how much influence we can have on a student's learning.

Daniel Coyle, author of *The Talent Code*, recently looked at a new
study on feedback from teachers.[2] This study showed that one simple
phrase could boost student effort by 40 percent. I was shocked when I
read this, but in the back of my mind I was already guessing what the
phrase would be—and I was right on the money. See for yourself:

> A team of psychologists from Stanford, Yale, Columbia, and
> elsewhere recently set out to explore the question: What's
> the secret of great feedback? They had middle-school

teachers assign an essay-writing assignment to their students, after which students were given different types of teacher feedback. To their surprise, researchers discovered that there was one particular type of teacher feedback that improved student effort and performance so much that they deemed it "magical." Students who received this feedback chose to revise their paper far more often that students who did not (a 40 percent increase among white students; 320 percent boost among black students) and improved their performance significantly.[3]

What was the magical feedback? Just one phrase: I'm giving you these comments because I have very high expectations and I know that you can reach them.

That's it. Just nineteen words. But they're powerful because they are not really feedback. They're a signal that creates something more powerful: a sense of belonging and connection.

Yep. I knew it had to do with expectations and potential. As a high-school English teacher, my students always responded when learning was presented as a challenge. Specifically, a challenge that I "expected" they would reach. This phrase, and the effect of 40 percent more effort, is so important. Are we teaching pre-service teachers about simple things like this? Are we focusing professional development on boosting student-teacher relationships?

BACK TO DALE CARNEGIE'S WORK

Carnegie's book has many lessons for teachers and leaders: Simple reminders (like the one above) that can lead to deeper conversations, better relationships, and a stronger influence on students' learning. Let's look at ten phrases from *How to Win Friends and Influence People* that bring us back to the basics of teaching and learning.

If you want to be enthusiastic, act enthusiastic.

Ferris Bueller's teacher: not enthusiastic. Randy Pausch from *The Last Lecture*: enthusiastic! Who would you rather learn from? A teacher and leader's enthusiasm carries over to their students. It carries over to the learning. I always wondered why we focused so much on content during pre-service teacher training. The teacher should already be passionate about what they are teaching. If you aren't, then maybe you shouldn't be teaching. If you want your students to be pumped about learning, you need to first look at yourself and see what kind of enthusiasm you are bringing to the classroom.

Any fool can criticize, condemn, and complain, but it takes character and self-control to be understanding and forgiving.

Guess what? Kids are going to let you down. They are going to miss assignments, forget to read, fail your test, maybe even cheat. But don't adults let us down, too? Every great relationship must have forgiveness and understanding attached to it—otherwise your relationship is more of an agreement or partnership, not an actual relationship. Hold students accountable for their mistakes. Then forgive them and empower them.

The royal road to a person's heart is to talk to them about the things they treasure most. . . . You can make more friends in two months by becoming interested in other people than you can in two years by trying to get other people interested in you.

Talk to your students (or your teachers if you are an administrator) and find out what they are interested in and passionate about. Spend time crafting ways for them to explore their passions and interests. In doing so, you'll let them think of you as someone they can talk to and someone who can teach them what they want to learn. This is the essence of inquiry in our schools; it works because they care.[4]

There are four ways, and only four ways, in which we have contact with the world. We are evaluated and classified by these four contacts: what we do, how we look, what we say, and how we say it.

Do you come to work every day as a professional? Make no mistake about it, improving relationships is not about dressing like students and "getting down to their level." It's about being professional every day. Dressing the part, looking the part, and acting the part. I remember those substitute teachers that kids used to harass when I was in school. Their biggest flaw: not looking the part. It may sound silly to focus on this, but I believe it is incredibly important. We trust doctors that are in scrubs. We trust lawyers that are in suits. And we trust teachers that are professional each and every day.

I am very fond of strawberries and cream, but I have found that for some strange reason, fish prefer worms. So when I went fishing, I didn't think about what I wanted. I thought about what they wanted. I didn't bait the hook with strawberries and cream. Rather, I dangled a worm or grasshopper in front of the fish.

Do you bait your students with strawberries and cream? Do you focus on what interests you when you teach? Or do you understand that our learners want something else. Find out what engages your students (you can do this from conversations) and use it! Maybe it is something to do with technology, maybe it is a connection to something in pop culture—but whatever it is, use it to boost the learning experience. Great teachers find new ways every year of delivering content that would otherwise be stale.

People rarely succeed unless they have fun in what they are doing.

So simple. Yet, we often forget this in the world of standardization. Make sure you teach above the test. My good friend Steve Mogg and I taught English. At the end of the year, we had finished our fourth book with some type of mystery in it. We decided to put our students through a made-up CSI case for a week. We devised an entire backstory, and each day the students had to find more and more clues. The classes battled against each other to solve the mystery. It was a lot of fun. Oh, and they learned more that week than any other week during the school year!

Develop success from failures. Discouragement and failure are two of the surest steppingstones to success.

I firmly believe that successful failures are the key to growth in school and life.[5] I see this time and time again in and out of school. Do you allow time for your students and teachers to fail? Do you provide opportunities for them to learn from those failures? If not, you are missing out on one of the biggest influences on learning.

Inaction breeds doubt and fear. Action breeds confidence and courage. If you want to conquer fear, do not sit home and think about it. Go out and get busy.

What are you doing right now to positively influence the learners and people in your life? Are you waiting for something to change? Are you waiting for the right moment? Stop waiting.

Do something right now. You may fail. You may succeed. Either way you will learn and set a great example. Let's use the research at our fingertips to inspire our own teaching and leading. We know what drives great learning experiences: relationships. It is your choice as a teacher and leader as to how you build those relationships!

BUT COMMUNICATION IS ALWAYS CHANGING

One of the hard things about building relationships and communicating with students is choosing *how* to communicate. Face-to-face is usually a great way to build rapport and have meaningful conversations, but we don't always get a chance to have one-on-one conversations during class. Our students are also living in a digital world. They communicate heavily through technology, yet we often struggle with how to build relationships in a digital way.

The best thing you can do is give students a choice in how they communicate with one another in and out of your class. Also, give them a choice in how they communicate with you. There is no reason to dictate what the communication channels are going to be when those channels are always changing, evolving, and revolutionizing the way we communicate and collaborate with one another.

Twenty years ago (when I was in high school) cell phones were just breaking into mainstream use. My parents let me get one because I was driving, and they thought it would be good to have in case of an emergency.

I didn't use it to text anyone. In fact, I thought (along with many of the people reading this book) that texting was so silly when I first heard about it. Why would I want to take the time to "text" someone a message when I could just call them instead?

Flash forward five years from my first cell phone and all I did was text. Facebook had recently come into our lives, and now I would get in touch with friends by texting, instant messaging online, or writing on their Facebook wall. I rarely called someone unless it was my mom.

Five years later, and everything had changed once more. The iPhone. Twitter. Group chats. And today, my wife Snapchats me photos of our kids, I stay in touch with friends over Instagram, and share professionally on Google+. My siblings and I rarely text, but we do use group messaging platforms like WhatsApp over five hundred times a day. Communication is on demand through a variety of platforms on my phone, in my watch, or embedded into my car, house, and so on.

So, with all of this change, why do we limit how students communicate in our classrooms (and outside of our classrooms)? It's time to reassess how students communicate with each other, how they communicate with their teachers, and how they collaborate on authentic work using digital (and not-so-digital) tools.

As the Dale Carnegie quote mentioned above, don't use strawberries and cream when a worm would work better. Take time to give students a choice of what communication works for them, and then build on that to create great relationships and collaboration between students and teachers.

A STEP-BY-STEP GUIDE: CHOICE IN COMMUNICATION AND COLLABORATION

1. SURVEY

First, give out a survey to your students at the beginning of the school year or new semester. With younger students, this survey can be done informally. The survey should include questions about what type of communicator they are as individuals and what communication tools they use the most in their everyday lives. Again, this will change depending on age and grade level.

2. REVIEW

You should review the results as an entire class. Pull out trends and show where the high percentages are for a shared communication tool. For example, when I did this with my students a few years ago, Twitter was the top communication tool that students used on a daily basis. But we did not immediately choose Twitter as our class communication tool.

3. DISCUSS

Discuss as a class what communication tools they would like to use for each of the following purposes:

- Teacher-to-class communication. Is this through a texting platform like Remind? Or a social network? Or maybe through a learning management system? Or just email?

- Student-to-student communication. Set expectations of what this communication should look like. Again, what is the main platform that the class will use?
- Student group-work communication and collaboration. How will students best collaborate with each other in group situations? What platform or communication tool works best?

4. EXPECTATIONS AND GUIDELINES

In this step, you need to create common communication and collaboration expectations and guidelines for students. Then allow choice to take over in the tools that they use. An example of guidelines would look like this:

- Students will choose the best platform or tool to stay up to date on class assignments, updates, due dates, and schedules. If this communication platform or tool is not working properly, they will let the teacher know immediately.
- Students will choose the best platform or tool that works for them and their classmates when working together. This choice will be discussed in their first meeting time and will be used throughout the process. If this communication platform or tool is not working properly, they will let their classmate know immediately.

This type of set guidelines allows for choices to be made in communication tools and how students collaborate with one another.

5. ITERATE

I made the mistake of allowing my students to choose their communication and collaboration tools like it was the wild, wild west. After three weeks, it was complete chaos. Groups were fighting over what tool they wanted to use and complaining about not receiving information that they needed.

When we decided to start using an LMS (learning management system) (examples include: Google Classroom, Seesaw, Schoology, Edmodo, Canvas, Blackboard, Moodle) as our hub for communication, it eased a lot of this in-fighting over communication. What I learned was my students wanted choice, but they were also fine with that choice being limited to a degree. With the LMS, we had a hub that they could all access and rely on for information. That allowed other students to use secondary forms of communication to work and collaborate. Without a chosen hub we were a bit lost, and that is why iteration is so important. Not only does technology change, but people also change how they work.

6. FACE-TO-FACE INTERACTION

The sixth and final step is the most important. Don't make all communication and collaboration digital. As much as possible, give real face-to-face interaction the most time in your classes. Regardless of whether or not students live in a "digital world," they still enjoy the social aspect of learning together and working with each other in real group situations.

Do not forget the influence that we (as teachers and leaders) have on our students. The same can be said for the influence students have on one another. A great classroom functions as a team. Have common goals, common language, and common expectations of each other. Communication is one piece that cannot be forgotten or put to the side; it is just as important to give choice in communication as it is for content, assessments, and activities.

·12·

PACE

How to Make Sense of Flexible Time Frames

Bobby was an eleventh-grade student in my English class, and he was angry.

"I don't understand this project, Mr. J. What are we being graded on, and when is it due?"

I looked around at the class to see a handful of students just like Bobby. They weren't used to this. In their eleven years of school, the game had been simple. A teacher like me would tell them what they needed to know, give them some homework and classwork to gauge their understanding, and then review and test them on whatever concept they should have "mastered" by now.

"There is no grade, Bobby," I said. "I want you to learn whatever you want to learn and share your experience with the class."

Bobby turned from my gaze toward his backpack and muttered, "This is stupid" under his breath. I could sense the tension in the room, but I wanted to make a simple point to my eleventh-grade honors students: school isn't a game to be played and learning doesn't always need to have points attached to it.

If you've read my book *Inquiry and Innovation in the Classroom*, you may recognize this scene from when I introduced the "20 Percent Project" to my students for the first time a few years ago. I had many students like Bobby who were frustrated with the notion of learning for learning's sake instead of for points. Yet, I don't blame Bobby or any of the students I had for thinking this way. They've been taught since a very young age that school is a game—and if you follow the rules, it is easy to win.

I want to make this clear to teachers and parents right now: Teaching our kids to play the "game of school" will not help them later in life. Instead, it will teach them that learning is measured only extrinsically and failure is not an option.

THIS ISN'T A RACE

I recently read a piece by author and entrepreneur Oliver Emberton, "Life is a maze, not a marathon."[1] As I read his post, I substituted the word *life* for *school*, and doing that opened my eyes to a simple question: What are we teaching our students about life, through the process of school?

Here's what Emberton has to say:

> Imagine if life were a marathon.
>
> There's a start, a finish, and the faster you run, the further you go: The secret to winning a marathon is to knuckle down and keep going.
>
> Most of us treat life like this, but reality isn't so two dimensional. Real life has no signs, and no straight lines. There's just a maze of infinite options.
>
> Some paths, like some careers, take five times longer to get where you want. Some paths, like some relationships, are dead ends.

Are we teaching students that life is a marathon or a maze? If life is a marathon, then maybe our current view on school works, but if life really is a maze (and Emberton makes a good case), then we have to agree on this: working hard and following the rules is no longer good enough.

HOW TO SHIFT AWAY FROM THE GAME OF SCHOOL

It's very easy to criticize something like the "game" of school. We've all played it (or resisted it and been labeled failures) on some level throughout our lives. We play similar games in certain jobs and industries as well. Yet, the reality of work right now—and the near future of work—has completely changed what students will be doing once they leave our schools.

In Will Richardson and Rob Mancabelli's white paper, "Preparing Students for a New World of Work in the 21st Century," they make this argument:

> Schools were built for a time when access to knowledge, information and teachers was scarce, restricted to what we could find in our local libraries and communities. But with the advent of the Web and our growing abundant access to all of those things, the form and function of schools is now in question as the needs of our students begin to shift in some dramatic, important ways.[2]

They continue to make the case for five important shifts in the workforce: the rise of self-employment, the rise of rapid job switching, the rise of the robots, work becoming mobile, and the employee becoming their own brand. Each of these shifts make our past education system more and more obsolete.

So, it's becoming increasingly clear: Life is not a marathon, and school should not be one, either. And work is shifting in ways we can't truly predict, and students will have to navigate new choices.

Moving away from the game of school must start with parents and teachers. If we continue to set up the same learning patterns and experiences, students will quickly realize the best way to succeed in the school setting is to "play the game." To move away from the game, we have to make three shifts in the way we teach, and parents need to support these shifts.

First, we need to give students choice in their learning experiences and support them when they mess up and fail. I cannot stress this enough. The way we naturally learn is by experimenting, failing, and learning from our failures. Having only one opportunity to take an assessment is not a natural way to assess understanding or any sort of competency. Having only one way to assess is not natural. We learn differently. Let's respect that in the learning choices we give students.

Second, we need to teach students to treat challenges as opportunities. This mindset is so important and must be modeled by the adults as well. There will be challenges. Learning is not always easy—in fact it's usually difficult. But if we treat challenges as new opportunities, we'll also be preparing students to overcome those challenges once they leave our schools and go through the maze of life.

Third, we then can teach students how to make their own game—instead of playing in a predesigned one. Think of the successful people in our world or in your life. Most of the time, they redefined what success could be and what it could look like. Many of them did not wait for their turn or pay their dues. Sure, there was trial and tribulation and tough times. But they made choices to take a different path to success. They created their own game and changed the rules.

GIVING STUDENTS CHOICE IN THE GAME THEY PLAY

Our current system of schooling traditionally dictates the order of learning for our students and the pace at which they can learn and grow. We plan the entire learning path, we tell students how long the path will take, and we rarely give students a voice in how they get to the end of their path.

Then, all of a sudden, we want students to make a choice. A big choice: What do you want to do with your life? After high school, students have to choose what they are going to do. Are they going to college? Are they going to a trade school? Are they jumping into the work force? Are they going to start a business?

Students also get to choose how long it will take for them to accomplish each of these things. They get to pick the order. They can change the pace at any point in time.

As a teacher, it may be easy to throw our hands up in the air and say, "There is no possible way I can give students choice in the order of work that they do and their pace while still covering the curriculum and everything my school is asking me to do!"

And you would be right. And you would be wrong.

You are right in the sense that it seems impossible. But you'd be wrong, because there are some ways we can give students choice in the pace and order of their learning, despite the restraints we have placed on us from all sides.

Here are six steps that can take you from "hands up in the air" to "I can do this" as a teacher.

STEP-BY-STEP PROCESS: CHOICE IN PACE AND ORDER

1. FOCUS ON THE END RESULT (WHAT STUDENTS KNOW, UNDERSTAND, AND ARE ABLE TO DO).

This is crucial to making any changes to instruction. As a teacher, you need to clearly understand the learning outcomes for any particular unit or lesson. What does understanding look like, you may ask. I always go back to a quote from the Teaching for Understanding project at Harvard:

If a student "understands" a topic, she can not only repro-
duce knowledge, but also use it in unscripted ways. For
example, a student in a history class might be able to
describe the gist of the Declaration of Independence in her
own words; role-play King George as he reacts to different
parts of it; or write out parts of an imagined debate among
the authors as they hammer out the statement. These are
called "performances of understanding" because they give
students the opportunity to demonstrate that they understand information, can expand upon it, and apply it in
new ways.[3]

In the first three chapters of part 2 of this book, we showed how
students can demonstrate their understanding and abilities in a variety
of unscripted ways. When teachers and students both have a clear view
on what the learning outcome will be, then there is flexibility in how
to get there.

2. PLAN A FLEXIBLE PATH.

The traditional path to understanding in a unit of study looks something like this: the student reads the content, the teacher discusses the
content and reiterates key points, the student discusses the content
with peers, and the student often does activities associated with that
content that covers specific skills. At the end of the unit, the student
demonstrates mastery of that content (and the skills) by completing a
summative assessment.

Planning a flexible path gives the student a choice in how they
navigate away from this traditional approach. It also provides multiple
opportunities to differentiate by content, process, product, and environment. As Carol Ann Tomlinson says in her book, *The Differentiated
Classroom: Responding to the Needs of All Learners*, "A great coach
never achieves greatness for his team or himself by working to make
all his players alike."[4]

Give students a choice in how they get to an understanding they can demonstrate in unscripted ways. The path can be different and full of choices, as long as we are all headed to the same destination.

3. USE SELF-ASSESSMENT CHECKPOINTS.

The best way for students to regulate their own pace and order of learning is to have self-assessment checkpoints throughout the unit. Checkpoints can be put in place while planning a flexible learning path, or they can be called out at any time by a teacher.

The key is to get students to truly self-assess themselves without any fear of judgment by peers or teachers. We know that self-assessment and reflection is one of the most powerful factors of learning. Give students multiple opportunities to assess their own work throughout the unit instead of only at the end.

4. ALLOW FOR MASTERY.

Rick Wormeli's view on redoing work hit home for me on so many different levels:

> If we do not allow students to re-do work, we deny the growth mindset so vital to student maturation, and we are declaring to the student:
>
> - this assignment has no legitimate educational value
> - it's okay if you don't do this work
> - it's okay if you don't learn this content or skill
>
> None of these is acceptable to the highly accomplished, professional educator.[5]

One of the quickest ways you can give students ownership of their learning is to really focus on the learning as growth, not a fixed outcome. That can be started by allowing students to redo work, and retake assessments. Do you do that already?

5. ALLOW FOR A CHANGE IN PACE.

In the book, *Finding Flow: The Psychology of Engagement with Everyday Life*, author Mihaly Csikszentmihalyi makes this comment:

> If you are interested in something, you will focus on it, and if you focus attention on anything, it is likely that you will become interested in it. Many of the things we find interesting are not so by nature, but because we took the trouble of paying attention to them.[6]

We have this balance as educators. Students still do not yet know what they will be interested in during their lifetime, but they also have current interests worth pursuing. Allowing for a change of pace gives students the flexibility to dive deep into a piece of new content they find interesting. Or they can take a longer amount of time working on a project where they've found a flow. It also gives students the choice to move quickly through tasks or activities that they might not like but understand need to be completed in order to work on a project they are excited about.

6. BE OPEN TO NEW LEARNING AVENUES.

Each of these steps opens up the possibility of learning differently. The traditional path to learning does not necessarily work as well with non-traditional learners. Our students live in a world of constant distraction, on-demand information, and multiple types of content. Choice in pace and order opens up not only flexible learning paths but also completely new learning avenues that have not yet been explored.

·13·

TECHNOLOGY

A Piece of the Puzzle
(But Not the Whole Puzzle)

Why are you using technology? Or more importantly, how are you using technology to better the learning in your classroom or school?

The pandemic forced many classrooms to use technology in ways that replaced in-person learning with online learning. This happened quickly and without training. It was not planned, and we were not necessarily prepared for it.

If you are like me, then you've had your fair share of technology screw-ups. Projects that didn't make sense (but used the "tech" you wanted to bring in). Activities that were ruined by a crashing website or some technological problem. And of course, you've probably dealt with the students, parents, and teachers who want to do things "the old way" because that is what they are comfortable doing.

To make sure you are using technology with purpose, you must first "start with why." If your students understand the *why* behind your technology use, then the class will have a purpose and technological glitches and issues can be worked through. If they don't understand the *why*, then any small issue could turn into a major problem.

Here are seven ways that teachers are using technology for a purpose. I'm sure there are many other ways to use tech with a purpose, but these are some of my favorites.

1. TO COLLABORATE IN REAL TIME

Remember when Google Docs broke onto the scene? It was magic. Students were writing and sharing in real time, able to see what the other students were doing and saying while still working on their own part of the project or activity. Flash forward seven or eight years and now real-time collaboration is a must for most online software. This type of technology allows project-based learning to be monitored, documented, and done outside of school hours.

At the last school where I worked, we were using Microsoft OneNote (as well as the Google products) to collaborate in real time. Whether it is staff planning together, students working together, or a combination of both, this technology has so many learning purposes.

2. TO REFLECT AND SHARE

I used to have my students journal in their marble notebooks. And during certain activities (like Writer's Bootcamp), I still do. However, what's nice about having students journal online and share in the cloud is the ability for their classmates to see what they have to say.

This is why I suggest blogging throughout the year and not just as a project. Make blogging a part of your student's life and you'll be able to see which topics, ideas, projects, and activities really impacted them. Sometimes it may not be what you thought—and sometimes their simple act of sharing will bring the class together in ways you never could have imagined.

3. BETTER RESEARCH

After I finished writing my master's thesis, "Peace Education in the 21st Century," I talked with my mom about her writing process in graduate school. It sounded awful—she would have to go to the library, find a resource, read almost the entire resource, make copies of the pages she wanted to use, and then copy it into her typewritten document. When the first draft of her paper was done, she would literally cut out whole paragraphs (yes, with scissors) and rearrange them the way she wanted (hence "cut and paste"). Then the whole document would have to be retyped on a nonelectric typewriter.

Technology has certainly made research and writing simpler and more time efficient. I'm not talking about typing a question into Google; I'm specifically focused on searching journal databases like ERIC through places like EBSCOhost. A nice search phrase will turn up hundreds of peer-reviewed results that can be sorted many different ways (such as by date or by full-text article). Those articles that you choose can then be automatically scanned for your keywords, then you can read the specific parts you want. You can then use what is applicable with a simple copy and paste, and the proper citation is already set up and ready to go.

How often do we really teach students how to research in today's world? Or do we expect them to learn on their own like we did?

4. WRITE AND REWRITE

Using tools such as Google Docs, the new Microsoft Word, or Draft, students are able to write and edit on the fly. They can get feedback from peers and teachers and then choose whether or not to accept that feedback on their writing. This goes for presentation platforms as well (Google Slides, Prezi, and Microsoft 365 PowerPoint). Technology has changed the writing process in much the same way it has changed the research process.

The most important part of writing is the revising and editing. Yet, we often take it for granted. Instead let's use the technology to track what types of changes students have made and if they are making the same mistakes in their writing over and over again. That way, the rewriting process can have a direct impact on how much they improve and change some of their writing habits over time.

5. MAKE SOMETHING (THAT MATTERS)

This may be my favorite way to use technology with a purpose. Students now have the ability to make movies, songs, pieces of art, websites, apps, games, and much more with technology. However, too often we ask students to make something that does not matter. We ask them to make a movie or poster or presentation that has no direct impact on the world around them.

Instead, let's challenge ourselves to start making technology matter. Make iMovies that can be uploaded to YouTube and have a purpose. Make games with a meaning. Make apps that matter. Yes, there is a time for fun and games. But if that is all we use technology for in school, then we shouldn't be surprised when that is all students use technology for once they get out of school.

6. KEEP A DIGITAL RECORD

Digital portfolios are a must (as we looked at in chapter 9). Not because colleges will want and need them in the future (which is happening sooner than you think). Not because it is a cool way to show off what you've done in class. Digital portfolios are a must because they show learning growth.

The best way to show how much a student has learned is through a digital portfolio. You can look back over time and see what they've created, written, and done in school, and how that work has improved (and in what ways) throughout their schooling. When students know their work will be on display and recorded, they also take pride in what they do because it will last.

Ask yourself if you are making "digital fridge art" or something worth keeping.

7. MASTERY ASSESSMENTS

Think about the last time you gave an assessment. I'm sure you prepared students for it during class, gave them materials to study, and supported them during the assessment. However, there were definitely a few students who struggled on this assessment. What happened next? You could either give them a retake, give them another similar assessment, or say that was their only chance.

If you gave them a digital assessment, you'd be able to see exactly which questions they got wrong in comparison to the entire class. You could see how much time they spent on the question and if the answer they chose was way off base or close. You could tailor a new assessment based on just the problems or questions they got wrong and make sure they achieved mastery on those topics before moving forward.

There are many more ways to use technology with purpose, but these are a great place to start. The problem we often see with technology is teachers who believe it is something separate from their actual instruction. When we make technology "special," it does not reflect the real world where technology is an integral piece of work, relationships, and livelihoods. In order to use technology as a transformative learning tool, we have to look at it from a different angle than we did ten years ago.

DON'T PUT LIMITS ON SOMETHING THAT IS ALWAYS CHANGING

Technology is changing at an incredible rate right now. It's not progressing by 10 percent each year—it's actually doubling exponentially in many different areas. The iPad was revolutionary only a few years ago, and today sales are beginning to plummet. Wearable technology is beginning to take a place in the market. And by the time you read this, something else will have "revolutionized" education as we know it.

I've heard this question in various forms many different times: How is technology going to save education? Radio and TV were going to save education, but of course they didn't. They changed consumption from primarily reading or live-viewing to listening and watching, but the prediction that televisions would replace teachers in the classroom has yet to come true.

Computers and similar devices were going to save education. The internet was going to save education. In fact, it seems as though every time a new technology changes our way of life, we believe it is going to save education.

Let's stop thinking about technology as a cure or savior for education. Instead, let's realize that great learning experiences have always had similar patterns and pedagogical strategies—and technology can be a part of that experience sometimes.

Let's also stop thinking about "ed tech" as something that needs a massive amount of training. Instead, let's understand that teachers, students, and parents are all on different parts of the technology continuum and will need varied support depending on their experiences. It doesn't matter if you are a digital native, digital immigrant, or digital explorer. Much of how you use technology will have to be learned through using it—not through training—because much of what you are trained on will change soon.

Let's stop believing that new tools will revolutionize education. Instead, let's understand that new tools often substitute, sometimes augment, and very rarely redefine the learning experience. It is how the teacher and students use these tools for learning that truly matters. And when technology is used to redefine a learning experience, the revolution is what the students make, create, and build with their tech—not in the many ways they can consume information.

A STEP-BY-STEP GUIDE: LET STUDENTS CHOOSE THEIR TECHNOLOGY

We've established the role of technology in education as something that must have a direct learning purpose. We've also made it clear that technology is not going to "save education," but how we use it can transform learning experiences.

Here's what this section is not going to be: a debate on BYOD (bring your own device). This is not about bringing your own device to school. This is about allowing for choice in the classroom when technology is available for learning purposes (regardless of how it got there).

What choice does to technology is bridge the gap between digital natives and digital explorers in the classroom. Students learn from students. Teachers learn from students. And students also learn a lot from teachers. Just because a student knows how to use an iPad to play games, watch Netflix, and listen to music does not mean they know how to use it as a true creation tool. This is what we can learn from each other if choice plays a role in how we use technology.

Technology can be used for almost every aspect of the learning experience:

- as an instructional tool
- as an assessment tool
- as a collaboration tool
- as a communication tool
- as a creation tool
- as a data tool
- as a writing tool
- and the list could go on and on . . .

1. THE PURPOSE OF TECHNOLOGY.

As a teacher, you must first decide on the purpose of technology in the learning experience. Are you using it for an activity, an assessment, or something else? Why are you using technology? How will it transform the learning experience?

2. HOW WILL TECHNOLOGY FIT INTO THE LEARNING EXPERIENCE?

Next, you'll have to decide if technology is going to substitute, augment, modify, or redefine the learning experience.

I recommend using the SAMR Model to decipher how you are using technology. SAMR is a model of tech integration designed by Dr. Ruben R. Puentedura, PhD, that is simple, easy to gauge, and offers all educators something to strive for.[1]

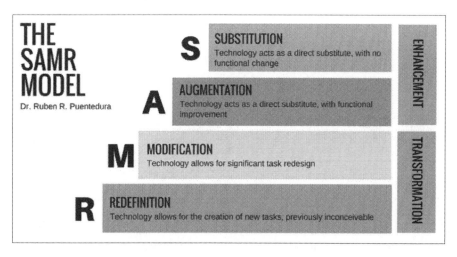

The goal, of course, is to get to the Redefinition level on the SAMR Model. However, sometimes you'll have to start with enhancement uses before reaching the transformative uses.

For example, using Google Docs to write an essay might be a necessary task your students have to complete. Google Docs's autosaving feature and cloud storage provides functional improvement over older word processing software (this would be at the Augmentation level).

If your students use Google Docs to collaborate in real time on the document in and out of class, then technology allows for significant task redesign from a traditional essay writing process (this would be the Modification level).

If your students then shared those documents with other peers around the world to get input and feedback on a position taken in the essay, we've now hit the Redefinition level where technology allows for a task that was previously inconceivable.

3. WHAT RELATIONSHIP DO THE STUDENTS HAVE WITH TECHNOLOGY?

You then need to find out what technology students already know how to use and what they are currently using in their own lives. How does this experience and technical knowledge fit into the learning objectives and purpose for technology?

4. PROVIDE A CHOICE IN TECHNOLOGY.

Next, you will give students the choice to pick an appropriate technology for the task. For example, if they want to make a presentation, they can choose between PowerPoint, Prezi, Google Slides, Haiku Deck, or hundreds of other presentation tools out there online.

You might be asking, "But why can't they all use the same tool or platform so it is easier for me to grade and learn?"

I made that choice many times as a teacher. I forced my students to use a specific tool or platform because I knew how to use the tool and would be an expert in the classroom. What changed my mind over time was a renewed focus on two things: what was best for the students and what really matters with technology.

What's best for the students is their ability to choose a platform or tool they either know how to use or one that they want to learn to use. This choice is significant (and we've gone over the same rationale in previous chapters) because it empowers the students' experience and gives them ownership in their learning.

What really matters with technology is not using the tool but how to effectively and successfully use technology for a learning purpose. That's why it's important to know how to use Excel or Google Sheets *and* understand how to use spreadsheet software for a learning purpose. The same goes for presentation tools, word document tools, and video editing tools. Learn how these programs, tools, and software function, and you'll be able to relearn a new tool for a transformative purpose, regardless of how much technology changes over the years.

·14·

STORY

A Powerful Way to Learn

Before he was championship coach and legendary NFL figure, Vince Lombardi was slated to be a priest. The son of a butcher, who had never played an organized snap of football in his life, the young Lombardi left Cathedral Prep two years early and accepted a scholarship to play high-school football at St. Francis as a nineteen-year-old. When he stepped on the field that first day, he realized something: he wasn't very good.

Then the injuries started. Between his time as a player at St. Francis and then in college at Fordham, "Butch" (as they called him) would spend a large majority of his time on the sideline or in the infirmary. It wasn't until his senior year in college that he became a starter and stayed on the field throughout a full season.

At five foot eight and 180 pounds, Vince was as undersized a lineman as you would find in the collegiate ranks at this time. Still, his two biggest detriments, a serious problem with near-sighted vision and a hot temper, became the parts of his game his coaches most admired.

Vince was a leader, first as a backup, and even more so when he got on the field. But his leadership failed to inspire as the team sputtered down the stretch, losing to rival NYU on Thanksgiving and costing Fordham a sought-after trip to the Rose Bowl.

Leadership problems persisted for Lombardi as he became a frustrated high-school coach and then an assistant at first Fordham, then West Point, and then the New York Giants. His big break came at age forty-six with the chance to coach the struggling Green Bay Packers.

The Packers were 1–10–1 for the previous season, and it seemed no one wanted this job. However, even as a first time NFL head coach, Lombardi had a confidence brewing inside of him that came from his belief in work ethic and commitment. Better yet, he believed those characteristics could transform the lowliest of teams.

Lombardi immediately went to work on changing the culture at Green Bay. His famous first line to the entire team, "Gentleman, this is a football," speaks to Lombardi starting from the fundamentals and always focusing on the principles of the game. Grateful for the opportunity to lead this team, Vince demanded longer practice hours, more time spent learning, and an incessant focus on the details.

Lombardi didn't stop with football. He wove together a new story about the Green Bay Packers. His players had previously been as scattered off the field as they were on the field. In Lombardi's first season as head coach, he redesigned, decorated, and brightened the offices and locker rooms. He changed the culture of travel by taking his players on better flights, staying at first-class hotels, eating high-end meals on the road, and dressing the part. Lombardi even paid for the team's now-famous green blazers they wore heading into away games.

He moved players' positions, benched veterans, and even traded their best player—a four-time Pro Bowler Billy Howton. The star wide-out, Lombardi said, was a bit too comfortable with losing. And that was something he would never tolerate.

Lombardi continued to talk about the Green Bay Packers in a different light at every opportunity. When he was hired, he told the board,

"I expect full cooperation from you. You will get full cooperation from me. I've never been associated with a loser, and I don't expect to be now. You have my confidence. I want yours."

As the board looked around, wondering why they had hired this guy from New York, Vince flashed a smile and finished his thoughts: "The Packers are steeped in tradition, and I expect, with plenty of hard work, to bring them back to the position they once held."

In his very first meeting with his quarterbacks that preseason, Lombardi took the players to a quiet locker room and pulled out a once-dusty blackboard. With chalk already in his hands, he leaned into the small huddle of men twice his size. "Gentlemen," he said, "we're going to relentlessly chase perfection, knowing full well we will not catch it, because perfection is not attainable. But we are going to relentlessly chase it because, in the process, we will catch excellence."

The 1959 Packers were an immediate improvement, finishing at 7–5. Rookie Head Coach Lombardi was named Coach of the Year. The fans appreciated what Lombardi was trying to do and responded by selling out every game for the 1960 season. Every Packers home game—preseason, regular season, and playoffs—has been sold out ever since.

In 1960, they narrowly lost the NFL Championship Game. In 1961, the Packers won the NFL Championship Game and went on to win four more titles in the next six years, giving Lombardi a total of five titles (including Super Bowls I and II) in his nine seasons in Green Bay.

Bill Curry was a twenty-two-year-old rookie offensive lineman in 1965 playing for the Green Bay Packers alongside such future Hall of Famers as Bart Starr, Ray Nitschke, and Herb Adderley. He shared a story of that day in Tiger Stadium when their team was losing 21–3 at halftime to the Detroit Lions:

> Curry sat there, in the locker room, frightened.
>
> Frightened of Lombardi.
>
> "Oh, my gosh," Curry thought. "This man is going to kill us."

The minutes passed and passed and passed, and Lombardi still hadn't entered the locker room.

The Packers got restless. They started to shift in their seats.

Lombardi then stepped into the locker room, wearing his famous overcoat. He didn't look the least bit angry.

"Men, we're the Green Bay Packers," Lombardi said. And he left.

Green Bay won the game 31-21.[1]

To this day, Curry, who later would go on to coach Georgia Tech, calls that moment the "best example of psychology" he's ever seen at halftime.

Lombardi had done what he set out to do: make the Green Bay Packers synonymous with winning and excellence. The story he crafted when he took over the losing team had turned into reality, and that reality carried their success forward.

THE SCIENCE BEHIND STORYTELLING

While many of us can see the benefits of stories in our daily lives and work, we often miss how important it is to achieve our goals. Lombardi understood this, but the science is particularly clear on the advantages of using story:

A 2010 study in the Proceedings of the National Academy of Sciences showed an intimate connection between the brain activity of speakers and listeners in conversation, demonstrating how the brain of an engaged listener "syncs up" with a speaker. By engaging students with compelling stories that impart important material, teachers reach students both emotionally and biochemically, increasing the potential for rich learning experiences.[2]

Sherrelle Walker—a teacher, administrator, and professor of thirty years—wrote about the science behind stories:

> Scientists have long known that human beings are storytelling creatures. For centuries, we have told stories to transmit information, share histories, and teach important lessons. While stories often have a profound effect on us due to emotional content, recent research also shows that our brains are actually hard-wired to seek out a coherent narrative structure in the stories we hear and tell. This structure helps us absorb the information in a story and connect it with our own experiences in the world.[3]

Stories provide a mirror into our lives and a window into the lives of others. Isn't that what learning is all about? We can do that with story.

Pamela Rutledge, a professor and director of the Media Psychology Research Center, puts it this way:

> Even with technology's increasingly sophisticated and jaw-dropping capabilities, the tools are becoming simultaneously more accessible and user-friendly. So much so, that the boundaries are blurring not just across technologies but also across the people who are creating, using, producing, augmenting, distributing, hacking, mashing, and every other "-ing" imaginable.
>
> In spite of all the excitement, however, the human brain has been on a slower evolutionary trajectory than the technology. Our brains still respond to content by looking for the story to make sense out of the experience. No matter what the technology, the meaning starts in the brain.[4]

The research has shown that stories fuel understanding of all types of learning objectives. If you want your players, students, or employees to understand principles, learn better, develop new ideas, apply theories, tackle real-world issues, innovate in their roles, then teach them with stories.

Leo Widrich, the co-founder of Buffer, explains that our brains can't help but function differently when we are being told a story:

> When we are being told a story, things in our brain change dramatically. Not only are the language processing parts in our brain activated, but any other area in our brain that we would use when experiencing the events of the story are too. And yet, it gets better.
>
> When we tell stories to others that have really helped us shape our thinking and way of life, we can have the same effect on them too. The brains of the person telling a story and listening to it can synchronize, says Uri Hasson from Princeton:
>
> "When the woman spoke English, the volunteers understood her story, and their brains synchronized. When she had activity in her insula, an emotional brain region, the listeners did too. When her frontal cortex lit up, so did theirs. By simply telling a story, the woman could plant ideas, thoughts and emotions into the listeners' brains."[5]

Anything you've experienced, you can get others to experience the same. Or at least, get their brain active, too.

A STORYTELLING SUPERPOWER

The short version of the science is this: Our brains pay special attention to stories, engaging more areas of the mind than when we hear or see facts. And when we learn a good story, our brains synthesize the neurochemical oxytocin. This helps us feel other's emotions and empathize with them.

Scientists have shown that high oxytocin levels lead us to donate more to charity, be more interested in people's well-being, and have more respect for others who aren't like us. Whether it is a friend, a coworker, a student, or an enemy, when we know each other's stories, we find empathy and learning in places we did not expect to find it.

STORY TAKES A LIFE OF ITS OWN

The legend of Lombardi grew as the wins piled up, but it was his presence and his locker room speeches that are still remembered today. They have taken on a life of their own, as the story he created about the Green Bay Packers that first year continues to live on not only in Wisconsin but also throughout the world by coaches who idolize him.

One of those coaches, Jimmy Valvano, has inspired millions of people during his life and after his battle with cancer. As a new coach, Jimmy V (as he is fondly called) was getting ready to give his first pregame speech. He was nervous and was looking for guidance on what to say and how to say it.

His idol was Lombardi, and while reading the book *Commitment to Excellence* he came across the story of Lombardi's first ever speech he gave in front of the perennial losers, the Green Bay Packers.

Lombardi waited and waited until there were only three minutes left before the game was about to start. Just then, he burst into the locker room. He walked back and forth, staring at the players, then said, "All eyes on me."

He said, "Gentlemen, we will be successful this year, if you can focus on three things and three things only. Your family, your religion, and the Green Bay Packers." They knocked the walls down, and the rest was history.

Jimmy wanted to do the same with his players. So, as his first game as the coach of Rutgers University's freshman team was about to start, he waited out in the hallway. His team was in the locker room.

With three minutes until the game, Jimmy went to knock down the doors just like Lombardi. Boom! They didn't open. He almost broke his arm. He was down on the ground; the players all looking at him.

He pulled himself up and started pacing, just like Lombardi. He knew what he was going to say, and kept whispering to himself, "Family, religion, and Rutgers University."

Finally, he said, "Gentlemen, all eyes on me." He paced back and forth before saying, "Gentlemen, we'll be successful this year if you can focus on three things, and three things only. Your family, your religion, and the Green Bay Packers!"

Lost in the intensity, the players were confused, and it took a moment for Jimmy to realize he had said Green Bay Packers, not Rutgers University. And that was how he started his legendary coaching career.

Jimmy V told the story of this pregame speech during the first ever ESPY Awards in 1993. Coach Jim Valvano's acceptance speech for the Arthur Ashe Courage and Humanitarian Award was the kind of moment that transcends sports. He took the stage battling terminal cancer and passed away shortly after in April of that year.

Although he had won the NCAA Basketball Championship as a coach and had lived up to Lombardi's standards of excellence, that speech is his legacy—and ours. His story, influenced by the story Lombardi created for his team, has lived on well past his death. His speech is replayed every year to raise money for cancer research and has impacted the lives of millions.

When we create a story, we don't know what life it will take on. We don't know the impact it will have. But, as the science and history points out, we'll have a much better chance at succeeding and achieving excellence if it is attached to a story.

We cannot forget this when crafting our own life story and especially when working with others to become better together. The story is just as important as the work that makes it a reality.

CHOICE IN TELLING THEIR STORY

In almost every classroom, in every subject and grade level, we ask students to tell stories. Sometimes, those stories are for language arts papers and essays. Often, they are for a history report. However, in almost every subject, we ask students to give or complete some type of presentation.

The presentation can be a daunting task for any student. Get up in front of the entire class and describe your learning. I've seen students break out in hives, faint, and cry many times during a class presentation. And I blame myself.

As a teacher, I want to see how my students can present an idea, event, or findings in a professional manner. Sadly, this usually ends up looking like a boring PowerPoint, filled with too many bullet points, too much text, and too few pictures. I sat through these types of presentations with my eighth-grade students before realizing what was missing.

A STEP-BY-STEP GUIDE: CHOICE IN PRESENTATIONS

We created a three-step process to prepare my students for presentations that I still use today when I get ready for my own presentations.

1. MAKE THE EXPECTATIONS OF THE ASSIGNMENT CLEAR BUT ALLOW THE STUDENT TO CREATE THEIR OWN WHY FOR THE PRESENTATION.

I'd generally recommend giving choice for the topic and assignment, but this isn't always the case. Usually, this is pre-built into our curriculum and the topic and assignment will have been created for the students. The presentation could be about the pyramids in Egypt, but I want to know why this is important. The students have to choose their own *why*, which is basically how they are crafting meaning from this topic and deciding what they want to share with the audience. If the student has a *why* and is not just listing facts, then we are on the road to a better presentation.

2. FOCUS ON HOW THEY TELL THE STORY.

It does not matter if you are presenting a lab report in science or on the Pythagorean theorem in math class—it's how you present the information that matters. When I first began focusing on the story aspect of presentations, my students began to call me out during class when I was teaching with a particular type of story. They learned the eight different types of presentations well by the end of the year,[6] but let's start with four that can be used at any grade level:

- **THE HERO'S JOURNEY:** Forced from the world they know, the character (which could be the student) has to move into an unknown place and go through a series of trials before being helped by a guide (this could be the internet or resource), finding success, and then coming back to their original place with knowledge that can help in multiple ways.
- **THE CLIMB:** Much like a TV series, the journey to a final result is long and arduous with multiple trials happening along the way. As they fight for knowledge and understanding, they begin to appreciate the journey itself, before a final climactic moment happens and the problem is resolved.
- **SPARKLINES:** The most famous presentation style has the presenter sharing the ups and downs of the journey. Presenting a dark reality with an optimistic view on what could be. Martin Luther King Jr.'s "I Have a Dream" speech is a great example of this style.
- **THE ACTION:** Start the presentation with the most interesting aspect of the work and catch the listener's attention. Then circle back around to the beginning to show how you got to that place. Think of how *CSI* shows the crime before going back and taking you through the story before the crime through what happens up to the final conclusion.

There are many different ways to tell a story in a presentation, and I would argue there is no "right way," but some work better for certain types of assignments. The benefit of presenting through storytelling is what we talked about earlier in the chapter: humans learn best through stories and experiences. By framing the presentation in a certain narrative structure, students create better connections with their audience, and they have the mindset of a storyteller instead of someone presenting a collection of facts and findings.

3. ALLOW STUDENTS TO CHOOSE HOW THEY PRESENT THE STORY TO THEIR AUDIENCE.

Throughout the rest of our students' lives, they will be judged on how well they present themselves. Their resume is a presentation. Their college and job applications are a presentation. Their interviews, proposals, and pitches are all presentations that will define the opportunities they will have in life.

When we tell students they have to create a PowerPoint presentation with ten slides, and what each slide will focus on, we are basically teaching them to *not* stand out. How many "death by PowerPoints" have you had to sit through as an adult? How many boring resumes and job applications have you seen? The world is filled with people who want to do things like everyone else does things. Let's not make that mistake in teaching our students. Give students choice in the following:

- The technology they use to present. Don't limit students to one presentation software. Let them use Keynote, Prezi, Google Slides, Haiku Deck, and the hundreds of other presentation tools that are available to use (for free).
- Setting the scene for the audience. Is the room dark or light? Are they giving handouts to the audience? Is there music involved? Allow them to be creative!
- Interaction with the audience. Is the presentation a stand-and-deliver-type of talk or are the students engaging

with their audience? Are they using technology to engage the audience? What other verbal or nonverbal cues are they using to generate discussion?

- Follow-up resources. What kinds of questions will their audience have after the presentation? How can they get more information? In what ways can you help reinforce this learning experience?

When you walk students through the choices they have in creating the presentation, delivering the presentation, and following up on the presentation, you will open their eyes to possibilities and questions they might never have even thought about during the process.

Above all else, these three steps put the presentation into a new context. It is not another assignment that they have to complete. It has a purpose, a focus, and lots of choice built into the process. Each step gives the students more ownership of their creative work and puts the power back in their hands of what to make and how to deliver it in the best way possible.

If stories are one of the most powerful ways to learn, let's make sure our students have the opportunity to tell lots of them and get better each time at refining their process and craft. They'll be presenting for the rest of their lives in one way or another, and it is our job to make sure they have a chance to stand out and speak up, regardless of the content they are presenting.

·15·

STRUCTURES

Creating Flexible Learning Paths

During the summer of 2020 as many schools were going back to in person, virtually, or some mix in between, a lot of teachers were faced with a new reality: teaching kids in the classroom and at home—at the same time.

This hybrid A/B model of schooling (it also goes by many other names) has a camera in the classroom to allow students to watch at home while some students are in the classroom. The students rotate days of being in person or at home. Technology plays a big role in making this happen, and it needs to work both in the classroom and at home for each student to pull it off.

Let's say that all the technology does work. In that case, the question I've been working on with teachers over the summer in PD and training has been: How do I structure the learning experience so kids at home and in class are both learning?

In this chapter I'll share four different models that I have seen work and that teachers are using around the country (and around the world) in hybrid A/B learning.

1. THE STEPS MODEL (I DO, WE DO, YOU DO WITH A TWIST)

This is (by far) the most traditional model of teaching that can work in a hybrid A/B environment. I usually start my training with this model to show how you can make the jump to hybrid teaching without changing too much as a teacher. Remember, we are all at different stages of the continuum, and in many content-heavy subjects, this model works well to get the students into a consistent flow of what the class will look like (whether they are in school or watching at home).

The following steps are adapted from The Reading Teacher's Top Ten Tools:[1]

S: SET-UP—PRACTICE REVIEW

You can do this with small groups or large groups, but for the sake of our interpretation, let's just say you have half the class in front of you in the classroom and the other half at home. You start by setting up the class for the lesson and doing some review of the previous day's lesson.

An important part of retrieval practice is having the students pull out their responses from yesterday's lesson instead of providing a review for them. This is also a good time to have students doing some practice or review problems or questions while you take attendance and complete the other beginning-of-class procedures.

When done well, students will come into class either in person or virtually with an idea of what the first five to ten minutes will look like every day. This also helps teachers see whether or not students are grasping the knowledge, skills, and topics that were covered in the previous lesson.

T: TEACH—EXPLICIT MODEL AND GUIDE OF NEW CONCEPTS OR SKILLS

The next stage is direct or explicit instruction of a new concept or skill, or a continuation from the previous lesson. This is the "I do" part of the lesson where the teacher explains and shares examples of what to look for, how to do something, and why it matters in the overall context of the subject.

There is little interaction in the *T* part of the lesson because students in class and at home are focused on understanding what the teacher is explaining. However, using a tool like Pear Deck or Nearpod can allow students to respond to prompts and questions easily throughout the lesson.

This does not have to be the teacher talking the entire time. Bring in videos, manipulatives, pictures, models, and anything else to help guide the student's attention and interaction with the content. It also does not need to be a long, drawn-out part of the lesson.

E: ENGAGE—PRACTICE WITH FEEDBACK

Here is where teacher-led practice comes into the lesson. The "we do" part of the lesson engages students in practicing the skill being taught in the lesson. There are a few ways you can do this in hybrid situations:

- Have students in class partner up with a student at home on their devices. This is a perfect use of a breakout room (in Zoom). As a teacher, you don't have to worry about monitoring the breakout rooms because they are happening in front of you.
- Students can do the practice individually or in groups using online collaborative tools such as Google Docs, Slides, Jamboard, or Padlet.
- Have students go through this process in class and at home with various students sharing on the in-class or virtual whiteboard.

P: PRACTICE ACTIVITY—EXTENDED PRACTICE OF NEW SKILL

The "you do" portion of the lesson has students practicing the new skill or engaging in the content by themselves. Here is a perfect time to have the cameras off at home and have students engage away from the device. Or, you can have them continue to use technology and share what they are doing and learning in your learning management system (Google Classroom, Seesaw, Canvas, Schoology, etc.).

My favorite part of this practice piece of the lesson is the ability for the teacher to work with an individual student or a small group who may need some additional help or who could use a challenge.

S: SHOW YOU KNOW—SHARE YOUR QUESTIONS

At the end of the lesson, you can bring all the students back together on the livestream (or have them do this individually, depending on your circumstances) and end the classroom in a similar fashion to how you started it. Have students show what they know and understand by answering questions, asking questions, and checking their own (and each other's) work. The goal here is for the teacher and students to have a formative understanding of their needs and where to go next (or what to tweak) in the following lesson.

Notice that in the STEPS Model, the students are *not* staring at a livestream the entire time. In fact, the only time they need to be on the livestream asynchronously is during the "I do" teaching and modeling mini-lesson part of the class. You have options for each of the other parts of the lesson on how to structure the learning experience.

2. THE STATION-ROTATION MODEL

The Station-Rotation Model is one of the most commonly used blended or hybrid learning structures, which has been implemented successfully by teachers all around the world pre-pandemic. You may have done this yourself with various forms of media and centers in your classroom. Now, with half the students at home and half the students in your classroom, the Station-Rotation Model still works, but it has to be adjusted accordingly.

The basics are simple to understand: each lesson has various learning stations that the students work through during the class period.

The easiest way to begin is to have two stations. Station one is instruction with the teacher. Station two is an online activity or assignment.

The teacher begins the class by explaining each station, then gets half the class (either the in-person group or at-home group) to start station two. The teacher then takes the rest of the class to station one for half the class period, before switching and taking the other half of the class through station one.

While two stations is the easiest way to begin, going into three stations may be the best option for station-rotation lessons long-term.

Catlin Tucker shared a perfect image to explain the three-station-rotation model in our hybrid A/B environments:[2]

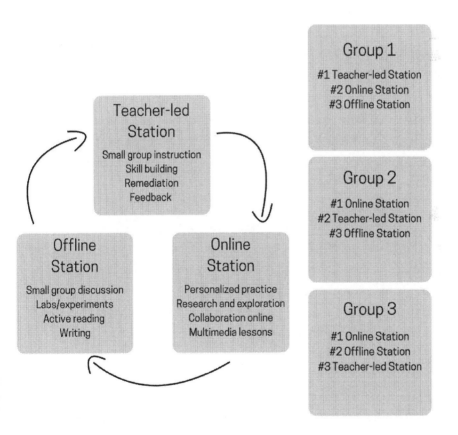

The class period is broken up into three distinct sections. For hybrid A/B learning, I would have all of the students at home in one group (Group 1) and break up the students in class into two separate groups (Group 2 and Group 3). However, if your situation is such that you have at-home hybrid students and full-time virtual students, that group may have to be split in two.

The Teacher-Led Station is what you will be leading (three separate times) throughout the class period.

The Online Station is personalized practice, research, exploration, or multimedia lessons that students can access on their own using digital tools and spaces.

The Offline Station can be used for some off-screen activities, getting students engaged in reading or other activities that they do not have to be logged on to complete.

The key to the Station-Rotation Model is to set clear time expectations at the beginning of the class and to keep them throughout the period. It also takes some serious planning. Don't be alarmed the first time (or second, or third) if both you and the students take some time getting used to this model!

3. CHOICE BOARDS

This is a self-paced option for the Hybrid A/B learning environment. The choice board allows for various levels of learning to take place and gives students choices in how they access information as well as demonstrate their understanding.

Tic-Tac-Toe Choice Menu:
Google Chrome PD for Teachers

Directions:
Start with number 5 and then make two other choices to make your tic-tac-toe. Remember to add notes to the Collaborative Notes as you go! Feel free to download apps and extensions you are interested in and play!
(CLICK HERE to Make a Copy and save to your Drive.)

1 **Explore** this database of Chrome apps and extensions to find ideas for you and your students. Share two of your favorites in the collaborative notes.	**2** **Explore** and search the Chrome Web Store Education Category for apps and extensions that will support learning in your classroom. Share two of your favorites in the collaborative notes.	**3** **Explore** this vetted list of Chrome apps and teacher reviews from Common Sense Media to find the best for the classroom. Share two of your favorites in the collaborative notes.
4 **Explore** this Google Chrome Pinterest Board to find ideas for you and your students. Share two of your favorites in the collaborative notes.	**5** **START HERE!** Watch this video: A Chrome Superhero. ⭐	**6** Using the Chrome App of your choice, create a **"Meet the Teacher,"** introduction. Share a link in the collaborative notes. (Suggestions: Canva, Flipgrid, Powtoon, or Google Slides.)
7 Create a **classroom procedures and rules presentation** using the Chrome App of your choice. Share a link in the collaborative notes. (Suggestions: PowToon, Google Slides, Animoto or Canva).	**8** Create an **interactive video lesson** for your students using EdPuzzle. Share a link in the collaborative notes.	**8** Create a **digital story** about a student that changed your thinking using the Chrome App of your choice. Share a link in the collaborative notes. (Suggestions: WeVideo, Storybird, Buncee, or Animoto.)

Created by Kasey Bell
www.ShakeUpLearning.com

149

Here are the steps you can go through to create a choice board in your content area:

1. Identify a unit, concept, or skill and what you want students to know, do, or make in order to demonstrate their understanding and proficiency.
2. Create or choose an assessment or performance task that allows students to demonstrate mastery.
3. List various instructional methods, resources, and strategies to prepare students for the assessment or performance task.
4. Choose four to six instructional methods to turn into choice-board activities. Each activity should be a similar length in time and cover common material. Here is where you can add different types of technology or hands-on experiences to the learning process.
5. Create a workflow for the students to follow. Have notes and formative checks as part of the choice-board design process. Allow for reflection during each activity.
6. Introduce the different choices to students and describe what the goals of the activity are as well as the assessment this is leading up to.
7. Let students pick activities based on their interests and needs.
8. As the teacher, a few of the activities or options might need more guidance than others. Make sure you aren't just "managing" this activity; instead, truly act as a guide and expert learner when the opportunity is available.
9. Once the choice-board activities are complete, put students into small groups to "jigsaw" their reflection. Bring students from different activities together to reflect on their learning experience and share. This can be a written, audio, or video reflection (think Flipgrid).
10. Listen to reflections and check the formative pieces for each activity to see if students are prepared for the assessment. If not, feel free to go through one more activity together as a

class or talk about any topics or concepts they did not understand during the activity.

11. Give the assessment or performance task.

12. **Bonus option**: Make your assessment into a choice board with multiple performance tasks that allow students to demonstrate an understanding of the content and skills.

As you can see, the process takes more time on the front end from the teacher, but you'll know that students are prepared for a performance task by going through this activity.

4. THE DISCUSSION MODEL

One of the biggest questions about hybrid learning I keep asking is: How do we continue to have student-centered learning experiences given the limitations of learning in the midst of a pandemic?

It's easy to jump straight to project-based learning, or maybe focus on a digital tool, app, or program. However, I often think it is best to start with the basics: let's get the students talking to each other and about relevant content.

Trying to have conversations on Zoom, Meet, or Teams can be trying at even the best of times. Add on the situation many teachers are facing with some students in front of them and others watching live from a device, and this becomes even more difficult. Yet, it can happen. It won't be perfect, and it will be different, but here are two ways teachers are getting the students talking during synchronous learning right now.

THE DISCUSSION GAME

My students rolled into class like any other day, and not much was changed. The tables were still set up in small groups, the projector was on with their "Do Now" activity on the board. And the homework for the week was written for each day. The only difference was that each seat had a white envelope filled with five cards of all different colors.

This was the opening of our first Discussion Game. I got the idea from my colleague Melisa Perlman and have seen variations of this game all over the place online. The best part about it is that it is simple to create, simple to explain, and completely modifiable depending on your subject, grade level, or classroom setting.

Simply put, each student gets a number of different colored cards to use throughout the discussion. They must play each card once but can play the question card multiple times after using all other cards.

<table>
<tr><td rowspan="7">THE
LIVE
(ZOOM,
GOOGLE
MEET,
TEAMS)
DISCUSSION
GAME</td><td>Pink = "I feel"</td><td>= 1 point</td></tr>
<tr><td>Green = "I think"</td><td>= 1 point</td></tr>
<tr><td>Blue/Yellow = "I know"</td><td>= 4 points</td></tr>
<tr><td>Red = a question</td><td>= 1 point</td></tr>
<tr><td colspan="2">✓ Each card may be "played" only once—except for red, which may be played any number of times.</td></tr>
<tr><td colspan="2">✓ To play a card, you must raise your hand and hold up a card.</td></tr>
<tr><td colspan="2">✓ After a card is played, it is put back in the envelope—again, except for the red one.

✓ All "I know" comments must be accompanied by specific references/evidence</td></tr>
</table>

Each card is worth a point, though it's completely up to you and your classroom or school if you want to grade this activity. The goal is to replace assessing only the final product (a quiz) with assessing the process of learning (having an active discussion).

This scaffolds the student-centered classroom in two ways. First, the game is centered on your subject, concept, content, or text for the lesson. Students have to be engaged with that content in order to respond with the answers and questions on the cards (I think, I know, I feel, I connect, etc.). Second, it models the many ways you can contribute to an active learning discussion. This helps the students who may be shy or want to hide during the discussion.

Additionally, we added a back-channel component to this game where students do not have to always talk out loud to the class to discuss and earn points, instead they can play their cards online in platforms like Canvas, Seesaw, Schoology, or Google Classroom as a way of participating in the discussion.

HOW TO MAKE THIS WORK VIRTUALLY

Now that you know how the concept of the Discussion Game works in a regular classroom environment, let's see how this can work modified for virtual and hybrid situations. I always share this process in my training, and teachers have used it all around the country in various K–12 levels.

First, all the students still have an envelope with each card. Or, if they are not able to have an envelope, they can write the color on index cards or color the index cards.

Second, the teacher describes how the game works. Students know that they are driving the discussion by showing a card they want to play either in person or on the screen via Zoom, Meet, or Teams.

Then it is time to play the game. The teacher facilitates by either calling on the students in the classroom or unmuting those students on the screen. Students are encouraged to keep their own score, and the teacher's goal is to get everyone involved and continue to mix up who is talking.

Finally, some students may not want to share their screen or talk online. They have the option to put the card they want to play in the chat, and then the teacher can call on them to share their comment, conversation, or question in the chat.

Teachers have modified this in all kinds of ways to make it work in virtual environments. Here are just a few examples:

THE FISHBOWL GAME

What's after the Discussion Game? The Fishbowl Game.

After playing the Discussion Game a few times, students began to get into discussions and own the conversation. Yes, they were prodded into giving answers and asking questions, but the goal of the Discussion Game is to get them talking (and to have me talk way less). It worked for our class and for many in our school, but it was not the final goal. I'd rather not have the carrot (or the stick) be the only reason students are talking, so we had to move away from that method. I also wanted to change up the format to one that was less scripted by the cards.

Enter the Fishbowl Game. This activity was used by my colleague Anthony Gabriele, and like all good things, I modified it to work with my group of students. There are some good write-ups online for the Fishbowl Game and many different ways to do it,[3] but I will explain how I did it in my class.

First, students are to have read, learned, or already delved into a specific text or content before the start of class. This, however, does not need to be homework. It could be learning that happened in a previous lesson or experience. The key is that the students are not learning something "new" during the Fishbowl; they are instead going to learn from each other during the discussion and share their insights and questions (much like in the Discussion Game).

Then you set up your classroom with two sets of circles. One big circle will be on the outside, and on the inside there will be a smaller circle of four to five chairs (depending on the class size, this could also be three or six chairs).

When students come into class, they will grab a seat. Don't worry where they sit, as all students will eventually get into the middle of the circle (the fishbowl) for the discussion. The students in the *inside circle* should be prepared to do the talking and discussing. The focus should be on having an active conversation using the techniques learned in the Discussion Game. The *outside circle* takes notes on the inner discussion. This could be scaffolded by the teacher to focus on specific areas of the conversation, or it could be more wide-open—like taking notes during a lecture. How you want to prep students for note-taking depends on your situation.

Jessica Vannasdall
@mrsvannasdall

From @ajjuliani class –FTW today Leading up to Socratic seminar, this game is teaching my ss how to interact. So many more ss engaged with purpose. We spent a lot of time with a TED talk b/f the game so they were prepared .SS said the content of the talk helped (social media).

The Discussion Game		
Try to earn as many points as you can during the discussion		
Yellow	"I think"	1 point
Green	"I feel"	1 point
Blue	"I know" with evidence	4 points
Red	"I have a question" Can be played multiple times	1 point

- To play a card, hold it up and wait your turn
- Once a card is played, record your points and return it to the envelope (unless it is red)
- You can play the red card multiple times
- All "I know" must be accompanied by specific references or evidence.

The Discussion Game		
Try to earn as many points as you can during the discussion		
Yellow	"I think"	1 point
Green	"I feel"	1 point
Blue	"I know" with evidence	4 points
Red	"I have a question" Can be played multiple times	1 point

- To play a card, hold it up and wait your turn
- Once a card is played, record your points and return it to the envelope (unless it is red)
- You can play the red card multiple times
- All "I know" must be accompanied by specific references or evidence.

Another option for the outside of the circle is for these students to be "coaches" for those inside the fishbowl. You can give a "halftime option" that allows the coaches to talk to and share insight with their peers inside the fishbowl.

Every five minutes, you'll want to replace the inner circle with new students. They can pick up where the previous discussion left off or start anew.

There are two keys to making this work. First, as a teacher, you must not prompt or get students talking. The goal is for them to have a productive struggle in the beginning and then get into a flow. Second, depending on your class, you may want to pick the fishbowl groups ahead of time to get a good mix of students for the discussion. This, of course, is your preference as the teacher.

Finally, you can assess this conversation in a few ways, but I'd focus more on the active discussion part than what was said at first. As you do it more often and students become comfortable, you can change a rubric to have different assessment pieces that reflect the content of the discussion.

As with the Discussion Game, you can add an online component to this as well. Have the outside of the circle write their feedback and notes in a shared document, a backchannel chat conversation, a discussion board forum inside an LMS, or any other way to make note-taking more collaborative.

HOW TO MAKE THIS WORK VIRTUALLY

The Fishbowl is a bit easier to modify for the virtual environment than the Discussion Game. The big change is that you aren't able to set up the classroom to look like a fishbowl. Instead, you have to make sure you only have those students discussing "inside the fishbowl" unmuted on Zoom while the rest of the students discuss and ask questions in the chat. Then, after a few minutes, you switch up who is having the conversation and unmute three to five new people to continue the discussion. You continue this process until all students have been in the fishbowl and discussed!

Each of these models works in any environment and is flexible for your unique situation. All of them can be modified for various grade levels and subject areas. So, what are you waiting for? Try it out and see which one works with your learners.

·16·

PURPOSE

What to Do When Students Struggle with Flexible Options

A teacher I work with asked me, "How do we deal with those students who aren't doing anything with their time when I give them choice? I feel like I've helped and helped, but they don't seem to care at all."

Maybe you've had this same experience with a student (or group of students) while running a choice-based activity or assessment in your class. Maybe it is something that worries you about starting this type of learning project where students get to choose their learning path and delve into their interests and passions. While inquiry-based learning may be scary (and exciting) for many students, it can also be difficult for a teacher to manage—especially when you've given students freedom when they are used to doing "nothing."

FREEDOM COMES WITH RESPONSIBILITY

First, let me set the context a bit. Since I ran a 20-percent-time project in my class a few years ago, teachers in my school district embraced the idea of choice-based learning. We had various teachers present on the benefits of this type of learning opportunity to our staff. And as a district we wrote "Genius Hour" into our language arts curriculum. Students at my school will hopefully be exposed to this project for the foreseeable future (or until we revamp the curriculum completely), and I am so impressed with the teachers' abilities to work with their students over the past two years.

Second, this question is not a new one. I'd be hard-pressed to find a teacher who has run an inquiry-based or choice-based project in their class and not dealt with some resistance from students. I've had many students who "pushed back" at first—either saying they didn't have anything to work on, or who wanted to use the 20 percent time to do work they had for other classes.

It is a difficult position for a teacher to be in. We've given students the "freedom to learn what they want," but with that freedom comes more responsibility than some students are used to. They no longer have the "reward or punishment" of traditional learning hanging over their heads, and for some, this gives them all the reason in the world to do nothing.

DON'T BLAME THE STUDENT

When this happened in my class, my first thought was to blame the student. I couldn't believe they would take the freedom to learn what they want and turn up their nose. Luckily, I quickly snapped out of that thought process. Blaming the student not only fails to solve this problem, but it also misses the entire point of inquiry-based learning.

I open every choice-based talk with the same three points:

- **PROBLEM #1:** Students are not allowed to learn what they want. Instead, they learn to play the game of school.
- **PROBLEM #2:** Students graduate or leave high school without knowing what they are passionate about or having a true purpose for learning other than grades.
- **PROBLEM #3:** The world is filled with many adults who hate what they do for a living and are only doing it to get by.

When a student chooses to do nothing with their time, it is not a complete "failure." It's merely their reaction to Problem #1. They've spent much of their schooling fighting for a grade, complaining about grades, or worrying about grades. Every paper, project, and assignment they've worked on has been crafted by a teacher (or a textbook) with guidelines, steps, and usually a rubric for evaluation. If you don't remember what it was like to be a student, let me tell you: it's exhausting. So, when a student "chooses to do nothing," resist your urge to be mad or upset and instead focus on getting to the root of the issue.

CHOICE NEVER FAILS

I was the type of student who loved to fly under the radar. I was completely content with getting Bs and sitting in the back of the class. I was friendly and didn't cause too much trouble, but mostly, I didn't want to be bothered with school. I often wonder how I would have handled the freedom we give our students during choice-based activities.

The three steps I've taken in the past (and try to help other teachers take) are based on my initial experience with this issue and how it reminded me of my own education experience.

STEP 1: TALK WITH THE STUDENT ABOUT LIFE (NOT THE PROJECT)

Have a conversation (or a few conversations) about life in general with the student who is doing nothing. It's simple, but something all the great teachers in my life have in common is their ability to talk with me. When I've noticed a teacher caring about me the person, instead of only me the student, I've responded positively.

The structure of inquiry-driven learning allows for teachers to talk with each student individually. Many students will want your advice on their project or ask you questions about their ideas, but some will shy away from this one-on-one conversation. Use this time to get to know your students better. For the student that doesn't want to work on anything, make it a point to talk about things other than the project and school. Share some of your experiences with him or her; it will make all the difference in forming a stronger connection.

Angela Watson shares a strategy that works, "The 2×10 strategy is simple: spend 2 minutes per day for 10 days in a row talking with an at-risk student about anything she or he wants to talk about."[1]

An article from ASCD shares the results based on the research of Raymond Wlodkowski. He reported "an 85-percent improvement in that one student's behavior. In addition, he found that the behavior of all the other students in the class improved."[2]

Angela was especially impressed by this anecdote:

> Martha Allen, an adjunct professor at Dominican University's Teacher Credential Program in San Rafael, California, asked her student teachers to use the Two-by-Ten Strategy with their toughest student. The results? Almost everyone reported a marked improvement in the behavior and attitude of their one targeted student, and often of the whole class. Many teachers using the Two-by-Ten Strategy for the first time have had a similar corroborating experience: Their worst student became an ally in the class when they forged a strong personal connection with that student.[3]

Try it with your students today, and see what happens in a few weeks.

STEP 2: ASK THEM FOR HELP

Most of the teachers in my school actually participate in Genius Hour by doing their own projects alongside their students. This is a great way to model the learning process, especially when we can share our "epic failures" with students. This also provides an opportunity to ask the student who isn't doing anything for help.

I would ask for help with little things—even something small and trivial. I'd also ask this student to video what the class is doing. You can ask them to record the progress of certain projects, and you can give them a few questions to ask each student on camera. Keep them active helping you and other students—because motion creates motion.

STEP 3: FIND A NEW PURPOSE

While passion and curiosity play a big part in my life, nothing inspires me to create and actually act more than purpose. As I mentioned above, the only purpose for learning in school this student has experience with is grades. They need to find a new purpose.

Have you ever thought about letting them make money with a Genius Hour project? I didn't until I tried it with one student, and they went into hyperdrive! This particular student told me he couldn't wait to get out of school so he could start making some real money. I told him that I like money, too.

We talked about what he would do to make money, and he told me that he currently made money designing T-shirts—bingo! He wanted to start his own brand. I asked why he didn't bring this up before, and he said, "They don't let you make money in school, man."

When I told him he could use this project to make his own T-shirt designs and sell them, he almost didn't believe me. When I hooked him up with a friend of mine who had recently started his own shoe company, he knew I was serious!

ADDING PURPOSE TO THE LEARNING PROCESS

When I ran the 20-percent-time project in my classroom, a few things were immediately apparent to me:

- My students had a hard time uncovering passion in the school setting.
- I had a difficult time helping them find their passion.
- Almost all of the successful projects had a driving purpose behind them.

Last year, as I helped out other teachers who were running inquiry-based projects like 20 percent time and Genius Hour, I always asked students what their purpose was in whatever they were working on. I explained that it's also what I ask myself when I'm working on something creative. Their purpose could be to change the world or make a video game that a thousand people play or start a band. But as long as they truly care about that purpose, they'll have the dedication needed to keep going when the process is difficult.

How often is the only purpose for learning tied to grades? How often is the only purpose for work tied to money? What happens to learners who don't care about grades and workers who want more from their job than just a paycheck? Chances are they stall out, fail to move forward, and move on to something else.

If we want creative students, we'll have to allow them to choose a purpose for much of their learning. If we want creative teachers and leaders, we need to allow for purposes other than financial compensation. The creative process cannot be forced, and it cannot be faked. It must contain purpose or it will never be realized.

A STEP-BY-STEP PROCESS: GIVING STUDENTS CHOICE IN THEIR LEARNING PURPOSE

If we go back to the "levels of engagement," you'll remember that an engaged classroom has two specific qualities: high attention and high commitment.

High attention can come from a variety of teacher decisions and actions in the classroom. You could be putting on some type of show, be funny, tell an interesting story, or craft a unique simulation or demonstration that captures the entire class's attention. While high attention is usually a mix of the environment and student buy-in, high commitment is intrinsic and must be connected to purpose.

1. DEFINE THE PURPOSE.

The first step to giving students choice in their learning purpose is to actually define that purpose on their terms. Yes, there are curriculum, content, and standards you have to cover as a teacher. But at the start of a school year or new semester, give students an opportunity to define and create three types of goals.

As an aside, with elementary students you may not want to go into as much detail with the career and lifestyle goals, but I do think it is important that students see their learning as connected to "who they want to be" and "what they want to do" when they are older.

Academic goals are directly tied to the type of learning they are doing in your class and at school in general, although they should not be limited by the particular class, subject, or grade level.

Career goals look forward toward a career. What career do they want to have, and what does success look like in that career? Students will often change career goals, and that is fine—I've changed career goals many times already!

Lifestyle goals focus on what type of life they want to live. This is not about money, but it could include money. Do they want to work seventy-hour weeks at a high-powered job, or work thirty-hours a week remotely while traveling? Many times, students need to be exposed to more types of lifestyles in order to understand the thousands of options.

2. CONSISTENTLY ASK, "WHY DO YOU WANT TO LEARN THIS?"

Once students have defined their goals, they have created a purpose for learning. Often the learning in the class will tie back to their academic goals, but hopefully it can ultimately tie back to their career and lifestyle goals as well.

Here's an example: A student has defined his lifestyle goal as traveling the world while working remotely thirty to forty hours a week. He realizes most of the work he'll have to do is freelance contract work for individuals and companies. His career goal is to learn enough freelancing that he could end up creating his own business that can run on his own terms. He is interested in building websites and apps as a potential business. His academic goals are to take classes that will help him gain the skills to build websites and apps in order to start freelancing while he is in college (if he needs to go to college). Work that he is doing in algebra, geometry, English, and physics can be directly tied to all three types of goals.

3. MAKE IT AUTHENTIC.

The third step is more for the teacher; it is asking, "How is this authentic or connected to their lives and goals?" We have the ability to take dry material and make it authentic. When you've taken the time to see your students' goals on display, it is hard not to take them into account while creating activities and assessments. You could stand in the front of the room, lecture from a PowerPoint, and drill facts and information at your class, or you could create the type of lesson, activity, or assessment that is shared in chapters 7–15. A student's purpose can only last for so long when they see that the class has little relevance to where they want to go in life. Make sure they see a connection and engagement will follow.

4. CREATE PEER ACCOUNTABILITY.

The key to this step is to understand that purpose-driven students are contagious. They inject life and energy into a classroom and subject. If another student's actions are prohibiting the class from reaching their goals, then peer accountability can handle it in ways a teacher cannot. This type of classroom environment is similar to a team environment at work or in sports. Each player or team member has their own goals and responsibilities, but they must work together for the benefit of everyone involved. When someone doesn't hold up their end of the work, the team needs to hold them accountable. Have students work in groups, and make sure they have shared goals along with their own personal goals. Positive peer pressure will take care of the rest!

When you've successfully taken these four steps with your class, a new type of learning will happen in (and out) of the classroom. Students will not only be engaged but they'll also care. They'll care about their learning, about their work, and about their place in helping the entire class move forward. The key is giving them a choice in defining their learning purpose.

The point here is simple: You don't need to create the desire as a teacher. Instead, our job is to help students connect their existing desires to this project as a new purpose for learning.

This is why choice never fails. Even when you think you've failed as a teacher. Even when that student spends their time "doing nothing," you've already succeeded in giving them choice. They may not take the choice and run with it right away. They may think this is a trick. They may not believe the freedom you've given them is real. But if you take the time to get to know this student, you may realize that this is a first step. The next time they are given choice, maybe they'll handle it differently. All we can do is support our students through this process as best as possible. We can't predict what type of impact it will have on their future, but believe me, it will have an impact.

·17·

YOUR ROADMAP

Putting It All Together

When *Atomic Habits* author James Clear shared the "Three Zones of Learning,"[1] I immediately started to think about our current situation.

1. **ZONE OF AUTOMATION:** Habits you have mastered.
2. **ZONE OF ADAPTATION:** Actions of just manageable difficulty.
3. **ZONE OF AGGRAVATION:** When the rate of change outpaces your ability to adapt.

How many of us have been spending time in zone three this past year? How many teachers have been living in zone three? How many school leaders and parents have also been in zone three?

Think about this in terms of a tennis match. Zone one would be like playing a match versus the ball machine or the coach sending the ball to the same forehand spot over and over again. At first, this may help you improve your swing, but very quickly you'll have mastered that shot from the same place and at the same pace. It will be automated—and there will be no improvement or learning.

Zone three would be like playing a match against Serena Williams. Every shot would force you to adapt your body, your racket, your position, your movement. She is so good, you would be consistently aggravated—and there would be little to no improvement or learning. It is difficult to learn when we are constantly forced to adapt in a reactive way, over and over again, beyond manageable difficulty.

I think about how these zones were also present in my classroom. When students came into the room (either on Zoom or in person), they were quick to open up their device, check the do-now activity, and get started with an entrance activity. Although the activities changed, my students were almost always in the zone of automation at the start of class.

Then there were times when I would put together a ridiculously hard or challenging assessment, and almost every single one of my students would be in the zone of aggravation. There wasn't much learning happening here either, just a lot of cramming for something they would often forget weeks or months later.

The sweet spot happened during design sprints and project-based learning experiences where students had a manageable level of difficulty but also an end in sight. Whether they were creating a PSA for a UN Global Goal or crafting a video with a student halfway around the world, these activities were in the zone of adaptation. It also happened during the smaller moments of teaching—a mini-lesson on the dangers of a single story,[2] a class discussion about passion versus purpose,[3] or an appeal's day.[4] The zone of adaptation is not about huge exponential learning gains; it is about small, 1 percent experiences that over time add up to powerful learning and growth.

Here's what James has to say about the power of tiny habits:

> So often we convince ourselves that change is only meaningful if there is some large, visible outcome associated with it. Whether it is losing weight, building a business, traveling the world or any other goal, we often put pressure

on ourselves to make some earth-shattering improvement that everyone will talk about.

Meanwhile, improving by just 1 percent isn't notable (and sometimes it isn't even noticeable). But it can be just as meaningful, especially in the long run.

In the beginning, there is basically no difference between making a choice that is 1 percent better or 1 percent worse. (In other words, it won't impact you very much today.) But as time goes on, these small improvements or declines compound and you suddenly find a very big gap between people who make slightly better decisions on a daily basis and those who don't.

Here's the punchline:

If you get one percent better each day for one year, you'll end up thirty-seven times better by the time you're done.

This is why small choices don't make much of a difference at the time but add up over the long-term.[5]

HOW DO WE GET 1 PERCENT BETTER EACH DAY?

When we look at what research says about becoming better at something, two pieces of evidence stand out. First, we must have clarity on what our goals are and where we want to go or what we want to become. Second, it is deliberate practice (combined with feedback loops) that increases the myelin in our brain and in turn helps improve performance and growth.

In this section, I want to talk about a process that we often miss when we look at learner success. We tend to talk about growth, goals, and instructional practice, yet we miss a key element of going from "defining a goal" to "achieving a goal" with our students.

It's about building better learning habits. We often talk about strategies but forget that our habits as teachers and leaders impact the habits of our learners. For example, students only become better at writing through deliberate practice and feedback on the practice. But if students do not have the habit of writing every day, it is extremely difficult to improve that practice and reach their writing goals. This is why tiny habits become essential in our adaptable schools and classrooms.

WHAT ARE TINY HABITS?

The 1 Percent Rule states that over time the majority of the rewards in a given field will accumulate to the people, teams, and organizations that maintain a 1-percent advantage over the alternatives. You don't need to be twice as good to get twice the results. You just need to be slightly better.[6]

Tiny habits can be used in our classrooms and schools in a variety of ways. I've seen how a daily routine and morning meeting can get kindergarteners ready for each day. I've noticed how a strong and daily anticipatory set (Bell Ringer, Take Five, Entrance Work, Do Now) prepares students for meaningful learning. I've witnessed teachers establish communication and collaboration norms so students understand what types of conversations are relevant to their learning. Each of these examples can be traced back to a habit that was developed in the classroom. And each habit can help build a better practice that is connected to a learning goal.

Here are ten habits that we can start doing right now with our students in order to help develop adaptable learners in flexible environments.

1. CONVERSATION AT THE DOOR, AT THE DESK, OR ON ZOOM

Talk to students about what's going on in their lives and they'll be more willing to come to you for help or guidance (and to take critical feedback). These short conversations spark the human and social aspect of learning that is an important piece to the puzzle. The key here is to do this with every student. The other key is to be authentic—kids are human beings and need us to treat them that way every day. This has to happen whether we are in person or online. The human need to connect is still a deep need regardless of location.

2. ANTICIPATORY SET
Traveling around the country, I've heard this called Entrance Work, Do Now, Bell Ringer, Take Five, and the list goes on and on. When I was in college, they called this the "anticipatory set," but who likes that name? Think about your favorite TV show, the first few minutes are full of action and catch your attention right away. That's what the first five minutes of a class should look like as well. Get 'em thinking!

3. ASSESS THE PROCESS OF LEARNING
Students tend to act like the rest of us and only focus on what is being measured (graded) and praised. Make the process of learning as important as the final product (a paper, a project, a test, etc.) and you'll see their work blossom.

4. WRITE EVERY DAY
You become a better reader by writing. Get students (and yourself!) in the habit of writing every single day. And make it enjoyable.

5. TRANSACT WITH VARIOUS TEXTS EVERY DAY
Just as you become a better reader by writing, you become a better writer by reading. It doesn't matter what subject or level you are teaching. Students need to have the daily habit of transacting with various (note the fact that these are various) texts each day. The daily practice allows students to make connections, go in depth with analysis, and find what they truly enjoy reading.

6. DEFINE PROBLEMS
We can't separate problem-based learning from the everyday learning that goes on in our classrooms. Make every day a problem-solving

day. The first step is to define problems and empathize with the issue. When students get into the habit of defining problems to their very core, they'll look for solutions that have the biggest impact.

7. COLLABORATIVELY WORK FOR A SOLUTION

Collaborative work must have a reason. Sitting students in a group and having them fill out a worksheet together is not collaboration. Instead, focus on the habit of solving those problems you've defined earlier in a group-type setting. This puts everyone on the same team with the same goal.

8. DEBATE

Get students fired up! The idea of a daily debate was first inspired by John Spencer, and I love this in the classroom. Set norms for how to debate, talk about what makes a strong argument, and have students voice their opinions on topics they care about. When it comes time to write that paper or give that speech, students will have a habit of making their case stand out.

9. CREATE, MAKE, TINKER, PLAY

Get students making each day may sound obvious, but this is hard to do without making it a priority. I've seen too many scripted curricula and programs that do not allow for any "tinker time." And when students finally do have this opportunity, they'd rather have a worksheet to fill out. Do this daily, and students will want to carry the making back home!

10. REFLECT

We all need to reflect more. It is one of the most powerful learning tools, to self-assess and reflect on what we've learned, done, and need to do. Have students reflect multiple times a day, and keep it short at first. "Taking a moment" will revitalize their minds and keep a daily practice of thinking about thinking.

Does this feel like too many habits? Start small. Try a few (or just one) in your class every day and then begin "stacking" the habits as you master the daily practice with one of them. Remember, these can also be combined in many ways, shapes, and forms, but the key is to do it daily and make it stick.

Whether we are crafting a new curriculum, adapting our current learning experiences, or planning for an unknown environment, one thing will remain consistent: this is hard work. There is no easy button in teaching and learning. And to go against the grain and move away from traditional practices is often lonely and scary work.

We are constantly faced with obstacles that get in the way of doing what we were meant to do. But they are there for a reason. As Randy Pausch said in his "Last Lecture":

> The brick walls are there for a reason. The brick walls are not there to keep us out; the brick walls are there to give us a chance to show how badly we want something. The brick walls are there to stop the people who don't want it badly enough. They are there to stop the other people![7]

Let's build a better learning experience for our students every single day, whether it is small or big, each change we make matters in the moment and in the future. I've seen these small changes have an impact in my life in many ways, most notably from my brother.

TINY ACTIONS WITH BIG RESULTS

Somewhere in Swaziland, a kid is going to school for the first time. She's got a new backpack filled with school supplies, a teacher excited to work with her, and a class full of peers ready to learn. She gets fed, challenged, and supported every day.

This happens, in part, because of my brother.

Somewhere in Pennsylvania, a family is battling a cancer diagnosis. They've been at the hospital all week, traveling back and forth. They are exhausted both mentally and physically. They haven't had a moment to do the daily work of running a household or preparing for the next week of school and work. When they get home on Sunday night, the fridge is miraculously stocked. The pantries are full of food. There are gift cards on the counter, and the entire house is cleaned top to bottom.

This happens, in some places, with help from my brother.

Somewhere in India a woman has been rescued and freed from a human trafficking ring. She is trying to put her life back and has to start somewhere. She's given a job at a local café that provides not only work but also counseling and support services to rehabilitate the mind and body each day.

This work is supported by my brother.

Growing up, we didn't think about many of these things. But life has a way of changing your perspective, your goals, and what we care about. My brother, Gabe, was born two years after me, which made us immediate growing-up partners. We did most things together. Whether it was playing baseball in the backyard, riding bikes around the neighborhood, making Rocketeer backpacks after watching a movie, or just listening to music, we hung out every day as many brothers do growing up.

He participated in all kinds of school activities, although our favorite was Color Day, a field day where every kid in the K–12 school competed against each other (we were Reds).

He played soccer, baseball, and basketball.

If you don't know Gabe, you may not realize that he has had to live his entire life with NF1. As a child, Gabe was diagnosed with neurofibromatosis, a disease where tumors grew on his nerve endings on the inside and outside of his body. He grew up getting MRIs, chemo, and surgeries on his eyes and his spine. He spent an entire year as an adolescent taking interferon treatments every day to slow the growth of these tumors.

I'll never forget watching him take shot after shot each night, pointing out to my parents where to put the needle because his legs were filled with bruises.

Gabe never defined himself by having NF. It was always present, and at times was impossible to forget, but he made it so there were hundreds of other reasons that could define who he was.

I've seen him make friends with almost everyone he has met. I've seen him destroy me in video games without a second look. I've seen him try out for a basketball team and deal with being cut by an awful coach, only to bounce back and take the positives. I've watched his intelligence shine through poker. I've seen my brother start his own business, pivot that business, and sell that business when the time was right.

But that was never a given.

Because of his NF, he had a learning disability growing up that made school challenging. We would always joke that school was for hanging out with our friends; we just had to do that learning stuff in between recess.

As we got older, I started to realize what a struggle school was for him. I'd finish my homework, ready to play, and he'd be working with my mom on problems for another hour. I didn't truly understand how hard that must have been until I became a teacher, and even more so when I became a dad with my own kids who all learn differently. Still, with the help of some amazing educators, Gabe continued to go through school, learning along the way.

One of the biggest hurdles to overcome at Jenkintown High School was the graduation project. The state had rules about what you could and could not do, and it was a mandatory requirement to graduate. My brother wanted to do something different; he wanted (for one of the first times I could remember) to shine a light on his disease. His graduation project idea was to start a fundraiser walk for NF.

The school could have said, "No, this doesn't fit within the graduation project requirements."

His advisor could have said, "Gabe, that is going to be a lot of work to pull off. Are you sure you don't want to try something a bit more doable?"

But . . . they didn't.

The principal supported the idea and helped make the connections with the township and police to shut down the streets. His advisor, Mrs. Klemp, was an educator who believed each child should pursue what they are interested in and passionate about while they are in school. She helped Gabe get the fundraiser over many hurdles and obstacles along the way. The entire community came together to support this fundraiser walk-a-thon. But, more importantly to me and our family, they showed up to support Gabe.

Someone who had struggled with school, Gabe was going to raise money for NF, lead a huge fundraiser that he put together, and graduate—headed to Shippensburg University.

I would ask him years later, "How did you pull that off?"

And he grinned and said, "It definitely wasn't just me. Have you met Mrs. Klemp? She loved me!"

In some ways, that walk-a-thon showed my brother's true colors. He always dreamed big and always wanted to help people. Despite growing up in hospitals, Gabe's passion for life was always present with friends and family. He was the kid that could have done anything with his Make-A-Wish opportunity, and he decided to take his entire family on a vacation—it was awesome!

After a year at college, he left to start his own business with a few friends. In fact, almost everything Gabe did after that point was entrepreneurial and in service to others (as you can see from his LinkedIn profile below).

Flash forward ten years later. Gabe had started a business, was working full-time, and had met this amazing girl (more on that later!). No one expected his next big diagnosis to be cancer. When

Gabe was diagnosed, Kristen was his girlfriend and soon to be fiancée. They quickly got married and began the journey of surgery and chemo together.

A year after this initial diagnosis of testicular cancer, Gabe and Kristen shared the great news with family and friends: the chemo had been successful. Gabe and Kristen were able to start working again and even take a long-overdue honeymoon as husband and wife.

After months of enjoying life together, working with the youth group, and beginning their life as a family—Gabe's health started to deteriorate. His right leg became numb, and then in April, a shooting pain shot across it that was unbearable. We rushed him to the ER to get treated and find out what was happening.

After many tests and consults with teams of doctors, they explained that Gabe's cancer was back, this time in many places. The cancer took form in a nerve sheath on Gabe's leg and spine. His L5, C3, and C4 were all deeply impacted by malignant tumors that took away movement and caused great pain. Additionally, the cancer was back in his liver and lungs.

Gabe, however, lived life as a chef, not a cook. He has always taken what life has given him and created something unique. I'm constantly in awe of how he did it. In fact, it challenged me in many ways to make life great every single day regardless of the circumstances.

Here he was, in the hospital with cancer, NF, shingles, and necrotizing fasciitis. Instead of feeling sorry for himself, he was sending many of us an email titled, "A Letter from My Heart."

That August, my brother passed away. He had just celebrated his thirty-third birthday with family and friends. But, in true Gabe fashion, my brother has not let death define his legacy.

While in the hospital, he and his wife talked about what he wanted to do when he got better. He wanted to help people that are helping others. Gabe had spent time in Swaziland, helping out kids and orphans that wanted to go to school. The Breathing Room Foundation had provided so much support to him and Kristen during their battle with cancer by giving them a stocked fridge, gift cards, and more while he was getting treatments. And his cousin was helping victims of human trafficking by running a café that provided jobs and support for their recovery. Each of these organizations meant something to Gabe, and he wanted to do everything in his power to help further their good work of serving people in need.

After his passing, Kristen and the family officially started Gabriel's Gladiators Foundation. The GG Foundation was started to honor those, like my brother, who fight bravely no matter what life brings and who live with courage and kindness in the middle of hard and difficult circumstances. In 2019, the GG Foundation raised over $22,000 for gladiators all over the world. Here are just a few of the gladiators the foundation helped support:

- One young man from Eswatini, Fanelo Zikhali, lost his hearing at the age of seven following a vicious blow to his head from a family member. He became completely deaf, but he continued to attend school, sitting in the front row and learning to read lips. Today, in a country that offers few services for people with disabilities, Fanelo not only survives, he thrives. As the owner of the Swazi Sign Language Training Center, he runs his own business, is an outspoken advocate for deaf rights, and has made his school a gathering spot of support for deaf Swazi people, offering them hope that they too can thrive despite their challenges. GG Foundation donations are helping Fanelo continue to reach out to some of the neediest people in Eswatini.

- A young woman from a large city in South Asia escaped from human trafficking and found work last August at the café that we support. In the café, she is offered safety, an opportunity to get an education, and a way to support herself and her family. If you met her, you would notice that she is often smiling as she serves coffee and food. She is small in stature but big in her desire to grow, change, and seek a better life for herself and her family.

- Rashid, a young man from the city of Philadelphia, still attends school when possible, despite the reoccurrence of his brain cancer. He and his large and loving family are refusing to be defined by the disease they are fighting and instead are working hard to support him and each other. The Breathing Room Foundation has contributed to helping Rashid and many brave children like him to continue to thrive despite a difficult diagnosis. School supplies, Thanksgiving feasts, personalized holiday gifts, spring/Easter baskets, dinners, and snack bags were all supplied by Breathing Room volunteers to him and others who face cancer with courage and hope.

Gabe's legacy lives on in the Gabriel's Gladiators Foundation, which was built, in part, by the family, friends, and teachers in his life that supported, challenged, and guided his journey.

You never know if one small conversation or decision can impact a life. And we also don't know how that ripple effect will impact the hundreds of others around that person. But we do know that each of us has the opportunity every day to make a positive impact during the small moments that don't get shared but always matter.

Keep making a difference, no matter how big or small it may seem at the time. As an educator, I thank you for the work you do every day, and as a parent, I'm indebted to the life-changing moments you will have on my own children.

Endnotes

CHAPTER 1

1   Lyn Hilt, "It's People, Not Programs," *Connected Principals* (blog), https://connectedprincipals.com/archives/339.

2   "Why Are We Still Giving So Many Tests?," A.J. Juliani (website), 6/1/21, http://ajjuliani.com/blog/why-tests/.

3   For simple, step-by-step guidelines for building curriculum, see Richard DuFour et al., *Learning by Doing* (Bloomington, IN: Solution Tree, 2006), and Mike Schmoker, *Focus*, 2nd ed. (Alexandria, VA: Association for Supervision and Curriculum Development , 2018), 1.

4   Rita Pierson, "Every Kid Needs a Champion," May 2013, Ted Talks Education 2013. https://www.ted.com/talks/rita_pierson_every_kid_needs_a_champion?language=en.

5   Gary Vaynerchuck, Instagram post, 4/3/2018, https://www.instagram.com/garyvee/?hl=en.

CHAPTER 2

1   Rudine Sims Bishop, "Windows, Mirrors, and Sliding Doors," *Perspectives: Choosing and Using Books for the Classroom* 6, no. 3 (summer 1990), https://scenicregional.org/wp-content/uploads/2017/08/Mirrors-Windows-and-Sliding-Glass-Doors.pdf.

2   Bishop, "Windows, Mirrors, and Sliding Doors."

3   A.J. Juliani and Erica Buddington, "A Backward Approach to Creating Windows, Mirrors, and Sliding Doors in Curriculum," January 18, 2021, in *The Backwards Podcast*, produced by A.J. Juliani.

4   Grant P. Wiggins and Jay McTighe, *Understanding by Design*, 2nd ed. (New York: Pearson, 2005), 16–17.

CHAPTER 3

1   Bill Murphy Jr., "Want to Raise Successful Kids?," *Inc.*, April 12, 2020, https://www.inc.com/bill-murphy-jr/esther-wojcicki-raise-successful-people-trick-weecare-youtube-23andme.html.

2   Esther Wojcicki, *How to Raise Successful People* (New York, NY: Houghton-Mifflin, 2019).

3   Jay McTighe, "What Is a Performance Task, Part 1," *Performance Task* (blog), April 10, 2015, https://blog.performancetask.com/what-is-a-performance-task-part-1-9fa0d99ead3b.

4   McTighe, "What Is a Performance Task."

5 McTighe, "What Is a Performance Task."

6 Jenny Anderson, "The Mother of Two Silicon Valley CEOs and a College Professor Shares Her Secret to Raising Successful Kids," *Quartz*, May 10, 2019, https://qz.com/1613252/esther-wojcicki-raised-two-tech-ceos-and-a-college-professor-whats-her-secret/.

7 Julia Harris Stern et al., *Learning That Transfers: Designing Curriculum for a Changing World* (Thousand Oaks, CA: Corwin: A Sage Company, 2021), 5–20.

8 Stern et al., *Learning That Transfers*. All images and figures used by permission.

9 Stern et al., *Learning That Transfers*.

CHAPTER 4

1 Nassim Nicholas Taleb, *Fooled by Randomness* (New York: Penguin Books, 2007).

2 Michelle Starr, "A Brief History of the QWERTY Keyboard," *CNET*, July 1, 2016, https://www.cnet.com/news/a-brief-history-of-the-qwerty-keyboard/.

3 Starr, "A Brief History of the QWERTY Keyboard."

4 Starr, "A Brief History of the QWERTY Keyboard."

5 Christopher Keep, "The Introduction of the Sholes and Glidden Typewriter, 1874," *BRANCH: Britain, Representation and Nineteenth-Century History*, accessed on September 16, 2021, http://www.branchcollective.org/?ps_articles=christopher-keep-the-introduction-of-the-sholes-glidden-type-writer-1874.

6 "Welcome to the Typewriter Museum," *Mr. Martin's Website*, accessed October 4, 2021, http://www.mrmartinweb.com/type.htm#olivetti.

7 Wikipedia, s.v. "Clarence S," last modified June 24, 2021, 6:22, https://en.wikipedia.org/wiki/Clarence_Seamans.

8 National Museum of American History, s.v. "Remington Standard No. 6 Typewriter," accessed October 3, 2021, https://americanhistory.si.edu/collections/search/object/nmah_850053.

9 Christopher Stokel-Walker, "6 Non-QWERTY Keyboard Layouts," *Mental Floss*, August 30, 2013, https://www.mentalfloss.com/article/52483/6-non-qwerty-keyboard-layouts.

10 Stokel-Walker, "6 Non-QWERTY Keyboard Layouts."

11 Herbert A. Simon, *The Sciences of the Artificial*, 3rd ed. (Cambridge, MA: MIT Press, 2019).

12   Robert H. McKim, *Experiences in Visual Thinking*, 2nd ed. (Boston: Cengage Learning, 1980).

13   "Design Thinking in K-12 Schools," Stanford d.school, https://dschool.stanford.edu.

14   "Our Method," Design Thinking at the University of St. Gallen, http://www.dthsg.com/program/.

15   A.J. Juliani and John Spencer, *The Launch Cycle: Using Design Thinking to Boost Creativity and Bring Out the Maker in Every Student* (San Diego: Dave Burgess Consulting, 2016).

16   Linda Tischler, "IDEO's David Kelley on 'Design Thinking,'" *Fast Company*, February 1, 2009, https://www.fastcompany.com/1139331/ideos-david-kelley-design-thinking.

17   "Attribution-NoDerivatives 4.0 International (CC BY-ND 4.0)," Creative Commons, https://creativecommons.org/licenses/by-nd/4.0/.

18   A.J. Juliani, "Using Design Thinking as a Leader," *A.J. Juliani* (blog), 10/19/2019, http://ajjuliani.com/blog/using-design-thinking-as-a-leader-a-practical-approach/.

CHAPTER 5

1   Simon Sinek, *Start with Why* (New York: Penguin Books, 2011), 71–72.

2   Tim Urban, "The Cook and the Chef," *Wait but Why*, November 6, 2015, https://waitbutwhy.com/2015/11/the-cook-and-the-chef-musks-secret-sauce.html.

3   James Clear, "Creativity Is a Process, Not an Event," *James Clear* (blog), accessed October 4, 2021, https://jamesclear.com/creative-thinking.

4   Michelle Lia, *Universal Design for Learning: Getting Started* (Leesburg, VA: NCEA, 2021), 18–19.

5   Katie Novak, "UDL vs. DI: The Dinner Party Analogy," *Novak Education* (blog), February 1, 2017, https://www.novakeducation.com/blog/udl-vs-di-dinner-party-analogy.

6   Allison Posey, "Lesson Planning with Universal Design for Learning (UDL)," *Understood*, accessed October 3, 2021, https://www.understood.org/articles/en/lesson-planning-with-universal-design-for-learning-udl.

CHAPTER 6

1   A.J. Juliani and Jay McTighe, "Everything You Need to Know About Backward Design and Curriculum Mapping 3.0," January 10, 2021, in *The Backwards Podcast*, produced by A.J. Juliani.

2 Dan Ariely, "Column: You Are What You Measure," *Harvard Business Review*, June 2010, https://hbr.org/2010/06/column-you-are-what-you-measure.

3 Jay McTighe, "Beware of the Test Prep Trap," Learning Personalized (website), March 24, 2017. https://www.learningpersonalized.com/beware-of-the-test-prep-trap/.

4 McTighe, "Beware of the Test Prep Trap."

5 "What Does It Mean to Learn?," What School Could Be, April 20, 2017, https://www.youtube.com/watch?v=g1HqedhOEfl&list=PLjFFPxvdS-vHlTKRcNJm38SBjicELHXJv&index=5.

6 Scott McLeod, "The Biggest Indictment of Our Schools Is Not Their Failure to Raise Test Scores," *Dangerously Irrelevant*, March 16, 2016, http://dangerouslyirrelevant.org/2016/03/the-biggest-indictment-of-our-schools-is-not-their-failure-to-raise-test-scores.html.

7 "Innovation Playlist: A Test of Value," https://www.youtube.com/watch?v=WOOCObPKCDk&list=PLjFFPxvdS-vHlTKRcNJm38SBjicELHXJv&index=6.

8 "Project-Based Learning Raises Student Achievement and Test Scores," School Outfitters, accessed October 4, 2021, https://www.schooloutfitters.com/article/project-based-learning-raises-student-achievement-and-test-scores.

9 Anne-Lise Halverson and Nell K. Duke, "Projects that Have Been Put to the Test," *Edutopia*, June 20, 2017, https://www.edutopia.org/article/projects-have-been-put-test-anne-lise-halvorsen-nell-duke.

10 Gallup Poll, *Creativity in Learning*, 2019, https://www.gallup.com/education/267449/creativity-learning-transformative-technology-gallup-report-2019.aspx.

11 John Larmer, "New Gallup Survey Shows Support for Project Based Learning," *MyPBLWorks* (blog), November 15, 2019, https://www.pblworks.org/blog/new-gallup-survey-shows-support-project-based-learning.

12 Will Richardson and Rob Mancabelli, *Preparing Students for a New World of Work in the 21st Century* (San Francisco: Bright Bytes), accessed September 27, 2021, https://www.westerncape.gov.za/assets/departments/economic-development-tourism/preparingstudentsforanewworldofworkinthe21stcentury.pdf.

13 Tim Hodges, "School Engagement is More Than Just Talk," *Gallup*, October 25, 2018, https://www.gallup.com/education/244022/school-engagement-talk.aspx.

14 Vanessa Vega, "Project-Based Learning Research Review," *Edutopia*, updated December 1, 2015, https://www.edutopia.org/pbl-research-learning-outcomes.

CHAPTER 8

1 Philip C. Schlechty, *Schlechty Center on Engagement* (Louisville, KY: Schlechty Center), accessed September 27, 2021, https://www.rcsdk12.org/cms/lib/NY01001156/Centricity/Domain/1053/sc_pdf_engagement.pdf.

CHAPTER 11

1 Lauren Liberante, "The Importance of Teacher-Student Relationships, as Explored through the Lens of the NSW Quality Teaching Model," *Journal of Student Engagement: Education Matters* 2, no. 1 (2012): 2–9, https://ro.uow.edu.au/jseem/vol2/iss1/2/.

2 Daniel Coyle, "The Simple Phrase That Increases Effort 40%," Daniel Coyle (blog), December 13, 2013, http://danielcoyle.com/2013/12/13/the-simple-phrase-that-increases-effort-40/.

3 Coyle, "The Simple Phrase That Increases Effort 40%."

4 Mifrah Rauf Sethi and Dr. Qadar Baksh Baloch, "How to Develop Self Confidence and Influence people by Public Speaking," *Abasyn Journal of Social Sciences* 6, no. 2 (1956), http://ajss.abasyn.edu.pk/admineditor/papers/V6I2-10.pdf.

5 For more on successful failures see Sethi and Baloch, "How to Develop Self Confidence."

CHAPTER 12

1 Oliver Emberton, "Life Is a Maze Not a Marathon," *Oliver Emberton* (blog), accessed October 4, 2021, https://oliveremberton.com/2014/life-is-a-maze-not-a-marathon/.

2 Richardson and Mancabelli, *Preparing Students for a New World*.

3 "Teaching for Understanding," Project Zero, accessed October 4, 2021, https://www.icyte.com/system/snapshots/fs1/9/0/a/6/90a619721974b234c7c6453acfeef5c9b4d653dc/index.html.

4 Carol Ann Tomlinson, *The Differentiated Classroom: Responding to the Needs of All Learners* (Alexandria, VA: Association for Supervision and Curriculum Development, 1999), 125–27.

5   Rick Wormeli, "The Right Way to Do Redos," MiddleWeb, September 25, 2016, https://www.middleweb.com/31398/rick-wormeli-the-right -way-to-do-redos/.

6   Mihaly Csikszentmihalyi, *Finding Flow: The Psychology of Engagement with Everyday Life.* (New York: Basic Books, 1997).

CHAPTER 13

1   Youki Terada, "SAMR: A Powerful Model for Understanding Good Tech Integration," *Edutopia*, May 4, 2020, https://www.edutopia.org/ article/powerful-model-understanding-good-tech-integration.

CHAPTER 14

1   Josh Robbins, "The Art of the Pep Talk," *Orlando Sentinel,* January 1, 2008.

2   Greg Stephens, Lauren Silbert, and Uri Hasson, "Speaker-listener neural coupling underlies successful communication," *PNAS,* (July 26, 2010), https://www.pnas.org/content/early/2010/07/13/1008662107. abstract.

3   Sherrelle Walker, "Using Stories to Teach," *The Science of Learning* (blog), June 14, 2012, http://54.186.226.228/blog/using-storie s-teach-how-narrative-structure-helps-students-learn.

4   Pamela Rutledge, "The Psychological Power of Storytelling," *Psychology Today,* January 16, 2011, https://www.psychologytoday. com/us/blog/positively-media/201101/the-psychological-power -storytelling.

5   Leo Widrich, "The Science of Storytelling," *Lifehacker*, December 5, 2012, https://lifehacker.com/the-science-of-storytelling-why-telling -a-story-is-the-5965703.

6   "8 Classic Storytelling Techniques for ENGAGING Presentations: Story Telling Methods," Sparkol (website), March 30, 2018, accessed September 27, 2021, https://www.sparkol.com/en/Blog/8-Classic -storytelling-techniques-for-engaging-presentations.

CHAPTER 15

1   Deb Glaser, "Planning the Small Group Reading Lesson," *The Reading Teacher's Top Ten Tools* (blog), September, 25, 2019, https:// readingteacherstoptentools.com/2019/09/25/planning-the-small -group-reading-lesson-teach-and-guide/.

2   Catlin Tucker, "Station Rotation in an Era of Social Distancing and Online Learning," *Catlin Tucker* (blog), June 21, 2020, https://

catlintucker.com/2020/06/station-rotation-in-an-era-of-social
-distancing/.

3   "Teaching Strategy: Fishbowl," Facing History & Ourselves, accessed
     October 4, 2021, https://www.facinghistory.org/resource-library/
     teaching-strategies/fishbowl.

CHAPTER 16

1   Angela Watson, "The 2x10 Strategy: A Miraculous Solution for
     Behavior Issues?," *The Cornerstone for Teachers* (blog), accessed
     October 4, 2021, https://thecornerstoneforteachers.com/the-2x10
     -strategy-a-miraculous-solution-for-behavior-issues/.

2   R. J. Wlodkowski, *Motivational Opportunities for Successful
     Teaching: Leader's Guide* (Phoenix, AZ: Universal Dimensions, 1983).

3   Watson, "The 2x10 Strategy."

CHAPTER 17

1   James Clear, @jamesclear, Twitter, July 24, 2019, https://twitter.com/
     jamesclear/status/1154032354463232001?lang=en.

2   Chimamanda Ngozi, "The Dangers of a Single Story," July 2009,
     TEDGlobal2009, https://www.ted.com/talks/chimamanda_ngozi
     _adichie_the_danger_of_a_single_story?language=en.

3   "Six Simple Strategies to Help You Find Your Passion (and
     Purpose)," A.J. Juliani (website), 7/17/2017, http://ajjuliani.com/blog/
     passion-strategies.

4   A.J. Juliani, "If We Have to Give Kids Grades, Let's Let Them Argue
     Their Merit," A.J. Juliani (blog), 9/21/2014, http://ajjuliani.com/blog/
     grades.

5   James Clear, "Continuous Improvement: How It Works and How to
     Master It," James Clear (blog), November 11, 2020, https://jamesclear
     .com/continuous-improvement.

6   James Clear, "This Coach Improved Every Tiny Thing by 1 Percent
     and Here's What Happened," James Clear (blog), accessed October 4,
     2021, https://jamesclear.com/marginal-gains.

7   "Randy Pausch's Last Lecture," Carnegie Mellon University,
     September 18, 2007, https://www.cmu.edu/randyslecture/.

Acknowledgments

A few years ago I wrote *Learning By Choice*. It was the second book I ever wrote, and I was proud because it could help people right away. The feedback I received from that book stuck with me as we headed into the first few months of COVID-19. In those moments, all I was looking for was practical and sound advice on remote, hybrid, and concurrent learning strategies.

The research on those practices led me to write *Adaptable*, and I have a long list of people to thank. First, I want to thank Erica Buddington and the Langston League for sharing their insights and wisdom with me on writing a curriculum that serves as a mirror. I have to say that Julie Stern and the entire Learning That Transfers team deeply changed the way I view the process of acquiring and understanding new concepts. To that end, both Catlin Tucker and Katie Novak provided such important step-by-step advice during the pandemic I consistently leaned on their work (and still do today).

I also want to thank the giants of this field. Folks like Jay McTighe, Grant Wiggins, and Heidi Hayes Jacobs for sharing their knowledge around curriculum and performance task development. Thank you, Esther Wojcicki for always being a guiding light into what drives real learning and curiosity in school and life. To Tim Urban, James Clear, and Trevor Ragan: you all consistently inspire me to write about topics that impact humanity.

To George Couros, Paige Couros, and the entire IMPress and DBC team, thanks for believing in me again and helping me throughout this process of writing a book!

Finally, to my wife, my five kids, and my family and friends. It takes a village, and I'm blessed with an amazing one!

About A.J. Juliani

A.J. Juliani serves on the faculty of the University of Pennsylvania Graduate School of Education (PLN) and was the former director of learning and innovation for Centennial School District. He currently provides keynotes, workshops, and curriculum development as the founder of Adaptable Learning (an INC 5000 Company in 2021).

As a curriculum coordinator, tech director, English teacher, football coach, and K–12 instructional coach, A.J. has worked toward innovative learning experiences for schools in various roles. A.J. is also an award-winning blogger, speaker, and author of multiple books, including the best sellers *Empower* and *Launch*.

A.J. Juliani brings a high-energy, fun, and engaging style of presentation through keynotes, full-day workshops, and online professional development offerings. His mix of personal stories from the classroom, real-world examples, and research-based insights lead to a learning opportunity for everyone in attendance. A.J. has worked at all levels of the K–12 spectrum and also has the lens of a parent—of *five* crazy kids.

Learn more about A.J. Juliani and his work at ajjuliani.com.

MORE BOOKS FROM

Empower: What Happens when Students Own Their Learning
by A.J. Juliani and John Spencer

Learner-Centered Innovation: Spark Curiosity,
Ignite Passion, and Unleash Genius
by Katie Martin

Unleash Talent: Bringing Out the Best in Yourself
and the Learners You Serve
by Kara Knollmeyer

Reclaiming Our Calling: Hold On to the Heart,
Mind, and Hope of Education
by Brad Gustafson

Take the L.E.A.P.: Ignite a Culture of Innovation
by Elisabeth Bostwick

Drawn to Teach: An Illustrated Guide to
Transforming Your Teaching
by Josh Stumpenhorst and illustrated by Trevor Guthke

Math Recess: Playful Learning in an Age of Disruption
by Sunil Singh and Dr. Christopher Brownell

Innovate inside the Box: Empowering Learners
Through UDL and Innovator's Mindset
by George Couros and Katie Novak

Personal & Authentic: Designing Learning
Experiences That Last a Lifetime
by Thomas C. Murray

Learner-Centered Leadership: A Blueprint for Transformational
Change in Learning Communities
by Devin Vodicka

Kids These Days: A Game Plan for (Re)Connecting
with Those We Teach, Lead, & Love
by Dr. Jody Carrington

UDL and Blended Learning: Thriving in Flexible Learning Landscapes
by Katie Novak and Catlin Tucker

Teachers These Days: Stories & Strategies for Reconnection
by Dr. Jody Carrington and Laurie McIntosh

Because of a Teacher: Stories of the Past to Inspire the
Future of Education
written and curated by George Couros

Evolving Education: Shifting to a Learner-Centered Paradigm
by Katie Martin

Made in the USA
Columbia, SC
31 December 2021

53091951R00109